Inspirational Quotes, Notes, & Anecdotes

That Honor Teachers and Teaching

To all teachers—past, present, and future. Yours is the greatest profession!
Thanks be to God for the teachers of the world.

—Garrison Keillor, public radio
personality, author, and humorist

Inspirational Quotes, Notes, & Anecdotes

That Honor Teachers and Teaching

Robert D. Ramsey

CORWIN PRESS
A SAGE Publications Company
Thousand Oaks, California

For information:

Corwin Press
A Sage Publications Company
2455 Teller Road
Thousand Oaks, California 91320
www.corwinpress.com

Sage Publications Ltd.
1 Oliver's Yard
55 City Road
London EC1Y 1SP
United Kingdom

Sage Publications India Pvt. Ltd.
B-42, Panchsheel Enclave
Post Box 4109
New Delhi 110 017 India

Printed in the United States of America.

Library of Congress Cataloging-in-Publication Data

Inspirational quotes, notes, & anecdotes that honor teachers and
teaching / [edited by] Robert D. Ramsey.
      p. cm.
Includes bibliographical references.
ISBN 1-4129-2679-3 (cloth) — ISBN 1-4129-2680-7 (pbk.)
      1. Education—Quotations, maxims, etc. 2. Teachers—Quotations. I. Title:
Inspirational quotes, notes, and anecdotes that honor teachers and teaching.
II. Ramsey, Robert D.
PN6084.E38I57 2007
370—dc22

                                2006002893

This book is printed on acid-free paper.

06 7 08 09 10 9 8 7 6 5 4 3 2 1

Acquisitions Editor:	Elizabeth Brenkus
Editorial Assistant:	Desirée Enayati
Production Editor:	Jenn Reese
Copy Editor:	Edward Meidenbauer
Typesetter:	C&M Digitals (P) Ltd.
Proofreader:	Joyce Li
Cover Designer:	Anthony Paular
Graphic Designer:	Lisa Miller

Contents

Preface

It's a Tough Time to Be a Teacher in America

Teaching has always been a tough task. But in America, it's getting tougher every day. Demands are high, pay is low. Expectations are escalating, while public support is drying up. Even parents are increasingly uninvolved, and litigation is now a common occupational hazard.

Unfortunately, through this stressful period, teachers can't count on anyone to back them up anymore; and their views are frequently ignored by decision makers. At the same time, teachers, at all levels and in all fields (especially special education), feel they are testing more, teaching less, and slowly dying from strangulation by regulation.

What bothers many educators even more is that pupils are increasingly ill mannered, rude, disrespectful, and, sometimes, downright dangerous. (School shootings were never part of the bargain before.)

Worse yet, resources are dwindling, school budgets are shrinking, and teachers everywhere are continuously being asked to do more with less.

To add insult to injury, teacher-bashing has become a national pastime. A growing number of politicians and self-proclaimed reformers have singled out teachers as the "bad guys," responsible for all the real and perceived ills facing public education.

For example, a former U. S. Secretary of Education compared teacher unions to "terrorist" organizations. And popular columnist George Will once described public education as a "national menace" and as "frightening as any foreign threat." (Does that sound like any teachers you've ever known?)

It's no wonder that many teachers are being stretched to the limit, some to the point of abandoning their careers. At the same time, few men and minorities are being attracted to the profession. Can a severe teacher shortage be far behind?

Obviously, teachers need many resources during trying times. But what they may need most isn't always money, materials, facilities, equipment, or supplies. They also need some old-fashioned respect, validation, recognition, inspiration, encouragement, and affirmation. So who is supplying these resources today? Precious few until now!

Inspirational Quotes, Notes, & Anecdotes That Honor Teachers and Teaching is a well-deserved tribute to the nation's most badgered, beleaguered, and belittled professionals. This long-overdue collection provides potentially career-saving homework for the soul of every teacher. It serves both as a wake-up call for teachers to press fiercely forward against odds, and as a voice of conscience for a nation that has too long neglected its most essential industry. Hopefully it can help replenish the nation's teachers and give them the grit to keep trying.

Easy to read and hard to forget, this little book may well be the quick fix every teacher is looking for to get through the day and to stay the course for an entire career.

Surprisingly, even though America's teachers are over-worked, overwhelmed, underpaid, and unappreciated, many are committed to sticking it out. These professionals aren't stupid or masochistic, so why do they put up with it?

The good ones are hanging on because in their heart of hearts, they know that theirs is still the most important job they can possibly imagine. Their lives matter and their work counts. Their rewards transcend economics.

What most teachers know—but sometimes forget—is that they are engaged in society's highest calling. Fortunately, the following pages are full of powerful reminders. Too many teachers today are frustrated, discouraged, depressed, and disillusioned. They need a boost. That's what this book is for.

ACKNOWLEDGMENTS

Like most publications, this book has many authors. Although my name appears on the cover, I am deeply indebted to many colleagues, associates, friends, and mentors who contributed quotes, ideas, inspiration, and encouragement throughout the creative process, including Debra Bower, Pam Canning, Joe Cavalers, Don Drayer, Owen Henson, Mike Homes, Jeff Jacobs, Carol Johnson, Carol Larson, Rollie Larson, Paul Schroeder, Michelle Simpson, Connie Skinner, T. J. Stelten, Elva Strang, and Bob Tift. If I have omitted anyone, it is due to faulty memory, not a lack of appreciation.

In addition, I am especially grateful to Elizabeth (Lizzie) Brenkus, acquisition editor extraordinaire, who guided me to and through this project; my wife and patient partner, Joyce; Nancy Herfert, lifesaver and word processing wizard; and all of the Corwin Press corps who helped to produce and promote this publication.

A simple "thanks," is insufficient. But it is all I have to offer. And I give it generously, profusely, lavishly, extravagantly, and wholeheartedly. There would have been no book without all of you.

—R. D. R.

Attributions and Tags

Quotations are slippery commodities. It's easy for them to get mixed up, misconstrued, or misattributed. Those of us who harvest and dispense other people's words cannot always be totally certain we have it exactly right. It is not entirely unheard of to find the same quote attributed to different sources in different collections. That's why every collection should carry some disclaimer, caveat, or apology. You're reading mine.

In compiling this collection, I can't unconditionally guarantee absolute perfection and accuracy. But I can assure readers that I have made every good faith effort to "get it right," to report each quote accurately, and to attribute all quoted material to the correct source.

Where possible, I have also attempted to add a tag to further identify sources by occupation, title, accomplishment, location, or time period. Unfortunately, this is not always achievable.

Consequently, there are some people quoted whom I know little or nothing about. I don't know who they are or what they did. But I do know they have something interesting, important, and worthwhile to say. So they are included. I trust you will allow me that license.

Likewise, not all those quoted are famous. Some only wish they were famous. Some are infamous. Others are flat-out unknown. Nevertheless, every quote has been selected on purpose for a purpose. I only hope you enjoy reading them as much as I did gathering them. And you can quote me on that!

—R. D. R.

About the Author

Robert D. Ramsey is a lifelong educator with frontline experience as a teacher, counselor, assistant principal, supervisor, curriculum coordinator, personnel director, associate superintendent, acting superintendent, and adjunct professor. He has served in three award-winning school districts in two different states, including the St. Louis Park (MN) schools, where every elementary and secondary school has been recognized by the federal government as a Blue Ribbon National School of Excellence. (St. Louis Park has also been identified as one of the top 100 communities in the nation for youth.) He currently works as a freelance writer in Minneapolis, where he and his wife, Joyce, can be close to their two grown children and four grandchildren.

Ramsey has earned substantial credibility as a spokesperson for the education profession through a successful track record of popular publications, including

- *501 Tips for Teachers* (2nd ed., Contemporary Books)
- *Well Said, Well Spoken: 736 Quotable Quotes for Educators* (Corwin Press)
- *Teacher Tips* (2001–2002 Teacher Book Club Calendar, Scholastic)
- *Lead, Follow, or Get Out of the Way* (Corwin Press)
- *What Matters Most for School Leaders* (Corwin Press)

Throughout his career as a leader of leaders, Ramsey has been an avid collector of quotes for educators. This current publication, containing some of the best from his collection, represents one of the most compelling arguments yet for honoring teaching as society's greatest profession.

Introduction: There's No Such Thing as "Only a Teacher"

You never hear anyone say, "I'm only an electrical engineer." Or, "I'm only a CPA." Or, "I'm only a dentist." But too many educators say, "I'm only a teacher." They're wrong. There's no such thing as "only a teacher."

Unfortunately, teachers are often their own worst enemies or detractors. Have you noticed that of all the people who downplay the role of teaching, many are teachers themselves?

It's not that teachers are more modest or humble than other people. It's that many suffer from a severe case of "only a teacher syndrome," a professional inferiority complex. It can be a self-fulfilling prophecy.

Respect begins at home. If teachers don't respect themselves or their profession, why should anyone else? Sadly, respect for educators is in short supply these days. Even—especially—among educators themselves.

In America, we desperately need to hang on to the good teachers we have and attract more highly qualified men and women into the profession. Of course, that can't occur unless teachers are made to feel special, needed, and worthwhile again. That's not happening today.

Too many of our teachers are stressed out, strung out, and wrung out. They need help to

- restore their resiliency,
- find new meaning in their work,
- energize their performance,
- rekindle passion for teaching,
- be reminded of why they became teachers in the first place, and
- have more fun on the job!

That's where this little book comes in.

Teachers matter. Someone needs to tell them that. And tell the rest of the population as well. The many voices in this collection make a powerful unified statement all teachers need to hear and that the rest of the nation should hear before it's too late.

Only a teacher? I don't think so. Being a teacher is more than a job. It is an honor, a sacred trust, and a profound privilege. Teaching is every society's most important work. Here are a few reasons why:

- Great teachers are necessary for a great nation.
- Behind all great men and women are the teachers who made them great.
- Even geniuses need teachers.
- Teachers are the nation's unsung heroes who get to see tomorrow's heroes before anyone else.
- Teachers have a ringside seat on the enchanted world of childhood. It keeps them young.
- Teachers change lives and see miracles happen every day.
- Teachers build tomorrow's "fond memories" today.
- Teachers impact generations of learners and have unforgettable influence.

The list could go on and on. But I rest my case. Teaching is the greatest profession. But don't just take my word for it. Read on!

The Quotations

It is a good thing for an educated man to read a book of quotations.

—Winston Churchill, British
prime minister, historian, and artist

Stealing someone else's words frequently spares the embarrassment of eating your own.

—Peter Anderson

Education
(Schools and
Schooling)

Education is always a hot conversation topic around the water cooler. People care about it. They have opinions about it. They praise it, criticize it, and argue about it.

And while others are talking about education, teachers are living it. They're where the action is.

People don't always agree on educational priorities or what constitutes a good education, but they all agree on its compelling importance. They just express it in different ways.

Following are some of the most interesting and insightful comments on schools and schooling from far-reaching times, places, and vantage points.

A good education is the next best thing to a pushy mother.
—Charles Schulz,
cartoonist (*Peanuts*)

The schools of the country are its future in miniature.
—Tehyi Hsieh, author
(*Chinese Epigrams Inside Out*, 1948)

I think education is power.
—Oprah Winfrey, actress, TV talk show host

The good school is that one in which in studying I also get the pleasure of playing.
—Paulo Freire, twentieth century Brazilian educationist

Education is the mother of leadership.
—Wendell L. Willkie, presidential candidate (1940s)

The best case for public education has always been that it is a common good. Everyone, ultimately, has a stake in the caliber of schools, and education is everyone's business.
—Michael Fullan, dean, Ontario Institute for Studies in Education, University of Toronto

The essence of our effort to see that every child has a chance must be to assure each an equal opportunity not to become equal, but to become different.
—John Fischer

There's something special about school, and it's something that needs to be encouraged more than it is.
—Terrence E. Deal, University of Southern California

Education is simply the soul of a society as it passes from one generation to another.

—G. K. Chesterton, British writer and critic

Good schools, like good families, celebrate and cherish diversity.

—Deborah Meier, educator

Public education is at the heart of what America does for the common good. Well-educated children and teens are an asset to all of society; everyone should contribute through taxes to the common goal of ensuring that education.

—Editorial, Minneapolis
Star Tribune, June 20, 2004

If we're serious about education in this country, we need to start giving teachers a living wage for their inspiring and tough work. If we're not serious about education in this country, we need to get serious.

—Daniel Handler, aka Lemony Snicket, author

Education is more than a luxury; it is a responsibility that society owes itself.

—Robin Cook, doctor and author (*Coma*, 1977)

Education is the vaccine for violence.

—Edward James Olmos, actor

If a nation expects to be ignorant and free . . . it expects what never was and will never be.

—Thomas Jefferson, U. S. president,
Declaration of Independence author

I don't think people who haven't worked in schools can comprehend the intensity of the work, the emotional involvement, the nonstop demands.

—Susan Moore-Johnson,
professor, Harvard University

In short, my little school, like the great World, is made up of Kings, Politicians, Divines, L.D. (LL.Ds), Fops, Buffoons, Fiddlers, Sycophants, Fools, Coxcombs, Chimney sweepers, and every other Character drawn in History or seen in the World.

—John Adams, second president
of the United States reflecting on
his early years as a schoolmaster

The whole purpose of education is to turn mirrors into windows.

—Sydney Jo Harris, syndicated columnist

The school is not there to raise your children.

—Elinor Burkett, author-teacher

As things are now, education is so cluttered and tangled up with a thousand senseless notions and stupidities that the task of reformation is almost a superhuman one.

—Walt Whitman, poet

When you ain't got no education, you just gotta use your brain.

—Kemmons Wilson, high school
dropout and founder of Holiday Inn

Education is the ability to listen to almost anything without losing your temper or your self-confidence.
> —Robert Frost, poet

The secret of education is respecting the pupil.
> —Ralph Waldo Emerson, author,
> minister (father of transcendentalism)

We all talk about how education is a priority. We all know it is, in fact, the basis of our future, yet we pay teachers like sh—t.
> —Stephen Blake, California legislative consultant

He who opens a school door closes a prison.
> —Victor Hugo, French writer

No teachers or administrator ever has to apologize for asking for money for education. If the community offered, the request would never have to be made.
> —Noah ben Shea, poet, lecturer,
> philosopher, and best-selling author

Education is the transmission of civilization.
> —H. G. Wells, British science fiction author

What a sculpture is to a block of marble; education is to a human soul.
> —Joseph Addison, English essayist

Educated men are as much superior to uneducated men as the living are to the dead.

—Aristotle, Greek philosopher,
scientist, writer, and teacher

Education makes a people easy to lead but difficult to drive; easy to govern but impossible to enslave.

—Edward Young

Separate educational facilities are inherently unequal.

—Earl Warren, Chief Justice, unanimous
opinion of the Supreme Court in *Brown
vs. Board of Education,* May 17, 1954

Education is leading human souls to what is best and making what is best of them.

—John Ruskin, British writer and critic

Sometimes, the hardest part of learning new things is unlearning old ways.

—Phillip C. McGraw (Dr. Phil),
TV talk show host and family counselor

The public, by and large, supports public education, but a number of the policymakers do not. I'm not a conspiracy theorist; I've never been to Roswell, New Mexico (where those aliens crash-landed, in UFO mythology). But the politicians who are beating up on us say we're failing. And, by their actions, they can set the system up to fail.

—David Jennings, interim
superintendent, Minneapolis, MN

Education is learning what you didn't know you didn't know.
—Daniel J. Boorstin,
Pulitzer prize winner, author

A good school is the price of peace in the community.
—Ursula Franklin, founder,
Ursula Franklin Academy

Education has really one basic factor, a sine qua non—you must want it.
—George Edwards Woodberry

Our progress as a nation can be no swifter than our progress in education.
—John F. Kennedy, U. S. president

A good deal of education consists of unlearning.
—Mary McCarthy, author

Upon the subject of education, I can only say that I view it as the most important subject which we as a people may be engaged in.
—Abraham Lincoln, U. S. president

Today's schools look much like Ford in 1926. The products they produce—student achievement levels—are not worse than they were 20 years ago . . . slightly better. But in the 20 years, the job market has changed radically. Just as the Model T that was not good enough in 1926, the education that was adequate for high-wage employment in 1970 is no longer adequate today.

—Murrane E. Levy, author, 1996

The gains of education are never really lost.

—Franklin D. Roosevelt, U. S. president

Any place that anyone can learn something useful from someone with experience is an educational institution.

—Al Capp, cartoonist

Ancora Imparo. (I am still learning.)

—Michelangelo at age 87, Italian sculptor and artist

Above all we take pride in the education of our children.

—Josephus, Jewish general and historian

Nine-tenths of education is encouragement.

—Anatole France, Nobel Prize–winning author

Public education is the link between our nation and our dream of liberty and justice for all.

—Elaine Griffin, National
Teacher of the Year, 1995

Education is forcing abstract ideas into concrete heads.

—Unknown

Schools are like a jigsaw puzzle . . . each piece has a unique design and cut that ensures just the right place to fit within the puzzle. Each morning, staff members . . . provide just the right place for every student to fit safely and securely.

—Karen Hegeman, author

The direction in which education starts a man will determine his future in life.

—Plato, Greek philosopher

There is no royal road to learning.

—Euclid, third-century Greek mathematician

We might stop thinking of school as a place, and begin to believe it is basically relationships . . .

—George Dennison

We have to abandon the idea that schooling is something restricted to youth. How can it be, in a world where half the things a man knows at 20 are no longer true at 40—and half the things he knows at 40 hadn't been discovered when he was 20.

—Arthur C. Clarke, science fiction author

The main purpose of education is to pass on the inherited wisdom of the race.

—John Adams, second president
of the United States

Establishing lasting peace is the work of education, all politics can do is keep us at war.

> —Maria Montessori, early childhood education innovator, founder of worldwide Montessori schools

[An] interest in education is one we could easily afford right now.

> —Rev. Jesse Jackson, political and civil rights activist

The schools aren't what they used to be and never were.

> —Will Rogers, humorist

Education is not filling a pail but the lighting of a fire.

> —William Butler Yeats, Irish writer

You can get all A's and still flunk life.

> —Marian Wright Edelman, author and founder of the Children's Defense Fund

To remove ignorance is an important branch of benevolence.

> —Ann Plato, African American poet, essayist, and teacher

To me education is a leading out of what is already there in the pupil's soul.

> —Muriel Spark, author

A good education is another name for happiness.

> —Ann Plato, African American poet, essayist, and teacher

Education is hanging around until you've caught on.
—Robert Frost, poet

If every day in the life of a school could be the last day but one, there would be little fault to find with it.
—Stephen Leacock, Canadian economist and humorist

Education happens when hope exceeds expectation.
—Andy Hargreaves and Michael Fullan, educator-authors

Education is the best provision for old age.
—Aristotle, Greek philosopher, scientist, writer, and teacher

Changing a school is like moving a cemetery.
—Unknown

America's schools miraculously have maintained and improved achievement during the last 25 years.
—David C. Berliner, Professor of Education, University of Arizona

It is not who you attend school with but who controls the school you attend.
—Nikki Giovanni, African American poet, essayist, and children's writer

Ignorance is no excuse—it's the real thing.

—Irene Peter, author

Without education, you're not going anywhere in this world.

—Malcolm X, civil rights activist

That's what education means—to be able to do what you've never done before.

—George Herbert Palmer,
American scholar and educator

Education is the chief defense of nations.

—Edmund Burke, British
politician, writer, and orator

Education: The path from cocky ignorance to miserable uncertainty.

—Mark Twain, author,
lecturer, and humorist

The public schools are America's children and require the continuing encouragement, nurture, and support of America's people.

—Ira Singer, professor, Hofstra University

Education—whether the object is children or adults, individuals or an entire people—lies in creating motivation.

—Simone Weil,
French mystic philosopher

No one can "get" an education, for of necessity education is a continuous process.
—Louis L'Amour, American novelist

⤬

[My family] believed in the public schools because they believed in a community. . . . My grandmother said, "Don't be a 10-dollar haircut on a 25-cent head." You avoided that by going to school and paying attention.
—Garrison Keillor, public radio humorist and writer

⤬

Non schola sed vita decimos. (Only the educated are free.)
—Epictetus, stoic Greek philosopher

⤬

A good education is not so much one which prepares a man to succeed in the world, as one which enables him to sustain a failure.
—Bernard Iddings Bell, chaplain, University of Chicago

⤬

If there were no schools to take the children away from home part of the time, the insane asylum would be full of mothers.
—Edgar Watson Howe, editor, essayist, and novelist

⤬

This classroom welcomes all, embraces chaos, supports everyone, and hopes that you find yourself better for having been here.
—Sally Huss, first-grade teacher, Minneapolis, MN

⤬

Excellence in education is the key to our nation's future. We must empower all our students with the best schools and guidance possible . . . we have a sacred obligation to put our children's needs first.

—Bill Clinton, U. S. president

In large states public education will always be mediocre, for the same reason that in large kitchens the cooking is usually bad.

—Friedrich Nietzsche,
German philosopher

If you are planning for a year, sow rice; if you're planning for a decade, plant trees; if you're planning for a lifetime, educate people.

—Chinese proverb

The beautiful thing about learning is that no one can take it away from you.

—B. B. King, musician

I want to thank God I live in a country where, despite so much rampant selfishness, the public schools still manage to produce young men and women ready to voluntarily risk their lives in places like Iraq and Afghanistan to spread the opportunity of freedom and to protect my own . . . even though so many days in so many ways we really don't deserve them.

—Thomas L. Friedman,
New York Times columnist and
Pulitzer Prize–winning author

More money is put into prisons than in schools. That, in itself, is the description of a nation bent on suicide.

—Jonathan Kozol, Rhodes
Scholar, best-selling author,
educator, and child advocate

Education: A succession of eye-openers each involving the repudiation of some previously held belief.

—George Bernard Shaw, Irish playwright

Schoolmasters and parents exist to be grown out of.

—John Wolfenden, author

My daddy used to ask us whether the teacher had given us any homework. If we said no, he'd say, "Well, assign yourself."

—Marian Wright Edelman,
author, founder of the
Children's Defense Fund

I call it "Kentucky Fried Schooling." Every school is like a franchise with its own separate sense of responsibility. But are you being empowered on the unessentials . . . rather than the things that really matter.

—Andy Hargreaves,
Boston College educator-author

We can't select our students. We have to take anyone who comes through the door. These are not children who go to charter schools. But our country was founded on public education. We shouldn't do anything to erode that.

—Gertrude Flowers Barwick, principal,
Holland School (Minneapolis, MN)

Schools need not be merely a place where big people who are learned teach little people who are learners.
> —Roland S. Barth, educational consultant, author,
> founder of Harvard Principal Center, and avid sailor

⚬>───<⚬

What we want for our children . . . we should want for their teachers; that schools be places of learning for both of them, and that such learning be suffused with excitement, engagement, passion, challenge, creativity, and joy.
> —Andy Hargreaves,
> Boston College, educator-author

⚬>───<⚬

Verily, you have more need of a good education than to win silver and gold.
> —Ali ibn Abi Talib, Islamic *Maxims for All*

⚬>───<⚬

My education was the liberty I had to read indiscriminately and all the time, with my eyes hanging out.
> —Dylan Thomas, Welsh poet

⚬>───<⚬

Education is the passport to the future, for the future belongs to those who prepare for it.
> —Malcolm X, civil rights activist

⚬>───<⚬

They know enough who know how to learn.
> —Henry Adams, historian (autobiographer)

⚬>───<⚬

Education is the process through which we discover that learning adds quality to our lives.
> —William Glasser, educator-author

⚬>───<⚬

Wisdom is not at the top of the graduate school mountain, but there in the sand pile at Sunday school.
—Robert Fulghum, author

Sign on a high school bulletin board: "Free every Mon. thru Fri.—knowledge. Bring your own containers."
—E. C. McKenzie, American humorist

Public schools are under unceasing attack, tax money is being channeled to competing schools—some of which operate with laughingly little oversight—and the best and brightest are abandoning ship. And "No Child Left Behind?" It's a joke.
—Nick Coleman, *Minneapolis Star Tribune* columnist

The problem with American education is a low ceiling of expectations. We have built schools that demand too little.
—Carroll Campbell, governor, South Carolina

Education is an ornament in prosperity and a refuge in adversity.
—Aristotle, Greek philosopher, scientist, writer, and teacher

If we force schools to do everything to everybody, can we protest when they don't do anything very well?
—Elinor Burkett, author-teacher

The classroom and the teacher occupy the most important part, the most important position of the human fabric.
—Unknown

True education makes for inequality: the inequality of individuality, the inequality of success, and the glorious inequality of talent, of genius.

—Felix E. Schelling, American educator

I look for a day when education will be like the landscape, free for all . . . the private school, the private art gallery have got to go. We want no excellence that is not for all.

—Elbert Hubbard, author-publisher

Education is too important to be left solely to educators.

—Francis Keppel, businessman and author

Education is not a product: mark, diploma, job, money—in that order. It is a process—a never-ending one.

—Bel Kaufman, German-born American novelist
and New York City school teacher for 20 years.

Education is teaching children to take pleasure in the right things.

—Aristotle, Greek philosopher, scientist, writer, and teacher

It is in fact a part of the function of education to help us escape . . . from the intellectual and emotional limitations of our time.

—T. S. Eliot, poet

We class schools, you see, into four grades: Leading School, First-Rate School, Good School, and School.

—Evelyn Waugh, author

To furnish the means of acquiring knowledge is . . . the greatest benefit that can be conferred on mankind.

—John Quincy Adams, U. S. president

Our best chance for happiness is education.

—Mark Van Doren,
professor, poet, and critic

Without teaching, there can be no learning. And without learning, there can be no advancement; not for individuals and not for society as a whole. Education is so important that this (almost) goes without saying.

—Randy Howe, special
education teacher and writer

Among the many purposes of schooling, four stand out to us as having special moral value: to love and care, to serve, to empower, and, of course, to learn.

—Andy Hargreaves and
Michael Fullan, educator-authors

The results of education are bitter, but the fruit is sweet.

—Aristotle, Greek philosopher,
scientist, writer, and teacher

Schools are change prone, but they are also change inept.

—Phillip C. Schlechty, founder,
Center for Leadership in School Reform

Abraham Lincoln once said, "He has the right to criticize who has the heart to help." So today, I say to critics of public education:

When you see something wrong, have the heart to help. But if you don't have the heart, please just get out of the way and let the rest of us get on with the job of improving our schools.
—Richard C. Riley, former U. S. Secretary of Education

⤝⟶⤞

The principle goal of education is to create men who are capable of doing new things, not simply of repeating what other generations have done—men who are creative, inventive, and discoverers.
—Jean Piaget, Swiss developmental psychologist

⤝⟶⤞

The elementary school must assume as its sublime and most solemn responsibility the task of teaching every child to read. Any school that does not do that has failed.
—William J. Bennett, former U. S. Secretary of Education, National "Drug Czar," and author

⤝⟶⤞

Arguably, the alternative to a student-centered classroom today isn't one that is teacher-centered but one that is legislature-centered.
—Alfie Kohn, educational theorist

⤝⟶⤞

A liberal education is at the heart of a civil society and at the heart of a liberal education is the act of teaching.
—A. Bartlett Giamatti, Yale University professor and former major league baseball commissioner

⤝⟶⤞

Education then, beyond all other devices of human origin, is a great equalizer of the conditions of men—the balance wheel of the social machinery.
—Horace Mann, American educator

⤝⟶⤞

Education is the companion which no future can depress, no crime can destroy, no enemy can alienate, and no despotism can enslave.

—Ropo Oguntimehin

Learning is good in and of itself . . . the mother of the Jewish ghettos of the east would pour honey on a book so that the children would know that learning is sweet. And the parents who settled hungry Kansas would take their children in from the fields when a teacher came.

—George H. W. Bush, U. S. president
and father of a U. S. president

If education is always to be conceived along the same antiquated lines of a mere transmission of knowledge, there is little to be hoped from it.

—Maria Montessori, early childhood education
innovator, founder of worldwide Montessori schools

These days, however, public education is under an all-out attack by forces that cynically want to use public funds to undermine public education.

—Nick Coleman, *Minneapolis Star Tribune* columnist

At the desk where I sit I have learned one great truth. The answer for all national problems—the answer for all the problems of the world—comes in a single word. That word is "education."

—Lyndon B. Johnson, U. S. president

There was, they argue, a time when our schools were better. Nonsense! There are more good schools today than at any time in the past. If there are also more bad schools it is because there are more schools trying to educate children who, in the good old days, would have been working in factories and sweat shops.

> —Phillip Schlechty, author and founder,
> Center for Leadership in School Reform

Education stands firmly as the cornerstone of our great nation ... their dedication and tireless efforts put forth by our educators to enhance the learning process is essential to the growth and prosperity of our communities and our nation.

> —Tom Ridge, first director of U. S. Homeland Security

It is not the IQ but the I Will that is most important in education.

> —Anonymous

I read Shakespeare and the Bible and I can shoot dice. That's what I call a liberal education.

> —Tallulah Bankhead, actress

The best thing for being sad, replied Merlin . . . is to learn something. That's the only thing that never fails. You may grow old and trembling in your anatomies, you may lay awake at night listening to the disorder of your veins . . . you may see the world devastated by evil lunatics . . . there is only one thing for it then—to learn.

> —T. H. White, author of *The
> Once and Future King*

Our schools no longer function primarily to teach . . . [Their] new role is best described as an amalgam of past surrogate parent, part chemical dependency clinic, part violence prevention center, and part drug enforcement agency.

—Gary J. Gustafson, small
business owner and former teacher

Education is not to reform students or amuse them or to make them expert technicians. It is to unsettle their minds, widen their horizons, inflame their intellects, teach them to think straight if possible.

—Robert M. Hutchins, professor,
dean, and president, University of Chicago

We're busy trying to figure out how to export democracy around the world. I'll tell you how. Give them a good public school system . . . when we're talking about why there's still democracy in this country after 200-plus years, it's no small part because we've had a public school system.

—David Jennings, interim
superintendent, Minneapolis, MN

An Old Man's Thought of School

And I see, these sparkling eyes,
Those stores of mystic meaning, these young lives,
Building, equipping like a fleet of ships, immortal ships,
Soon to sail out over the measureless seas,
On the soul's voyage.
Only a lot of boys and girls?
Only the tiresome spelling, writing, ciphering classes?
Only a public school?
Ah more, infinitely more,
And you America,
Cast you the real reckoning for the present?

The lights and shadows of your future, good or evil?
To girlhood, boyhood look, the teacher and the school.
—Walt Whitman, American poet (written for the
inauguration of a public school in Camden, NJ, in 1874)

Public instruction should be the first object of government.
—Napoleon Bonaparte,
military strategist, emperor of France

Everything America is or ever hopes to be depends on what
happens in our school's classroom.
—Frosty Troy, editor, *Oklahoma Observer*

When I was a boy on the Mississippi River, there was a
proposition for a township there to discontinue public schools
because they were too expensive. An old farmer spoke up and
said if they stopped building schools they would not save anything, because every time a school was closed a jail had to be
built.
—Mark Twain, author, lecturer, and humorist

As someone who has had the benefit of a Park High education and also sent his own daughters to public school, I know
all too well how valuable a quality public school system can
be. Our public schools are the backbone of our country. They
bring together the fireman's daughter with the businessman's son, children of all races, creeds, and color. And the
best of those schools forge these different strands into
communities.
—Thomas L. Friedman, *New York Times* columnist
and Pulitzer Prize–winning author

There is a place in America to take a stand: it is public education. It is the underpinning of our cultural and political system. It is the great common ground. Public education after all is the engine that moves us as a society toward a common destiny . . . it is in public education that the American dream begins to take shape.

—Tom Brokaw, TV news anchor and author

Students

For anyone looking for a reason why teachers put up with being overworked, overwhelmed, underpaid, and unappreciated, this is it—it's kids. It's the students. It's that simple.

Children truly are our nation's most precious resource. And like most societies, we entrust the safekeeping of these most valuable assets to a very special and select group of people. In America, we call them teachers.

Our society may not reward teachers handsomely, but it trusts them explicitly. That makes being a teacher a huge deal!

Children wake up fresh every morning, excited about the day and ready to be surprised. So do good teachers. A teacher never steps into the same classroom twice.

That's why the greatest fringe benefit of a career in teaching is the chance to participate in the parallel universe of childhood. It's a world of wonder and beauty that most people largely miss out on.

Teachers not only borrow children from their parents for a while, they polish them and return them brighter than

Children are like wet cement. Whatever falls on them makes an impression.

—Haim Ginott, teacher and author

The hearts of small children are delicate organs.

—Carson McCullers, author

There must be such a thing as a child with average ability, but you can't find a parent who will admit that it is his child.

—Thomas Bailey

All a youngster wants out of school is himself.

—E. C. McKenzie, American humorist

Some students drink at the fountain of knowledge, while others just gargle.

—Unknown

It is important that students bring a certain ragamuffin, barefoot irreverence to their studies; they are not here to worship what is known, but to question it.

—Jacob Bronowski, Polish educator

There is always one moment in childhood when the door opens and lets the future in.

—Graham Greene, author

Each student is a chapter in the greatest story I could ever hope to write. It is this that inspires me.

—Randy Howe, special
education teacher and author

The average four-year-old laughs or smiles four hundred times each day; the typical adult laughs or smiles fifteen times each day. Clearly we have much to learn about playfulness from children.

—Roland S. Barth, educational consultant, author,
founder of Harvard Principal Center, and avid sailor

Rarely is the question asked: "Is our children learning?"

—President George W. Bush, Florence,
South Carolina, January 11, 2000

You have brains in your head. You have feet in your shoes. You can steer yourself in any direction you choose.

—Dr. Seuss, children's author,
in *Oh, the Places You'll Go!*

Children are to be treasured like people who arrive from foreign countries, who must be gently instructed in the customs of ours.

—Ben Franklin, printer, diplomat,
author, and one of our Founding Fathers

If you want your children to keep their feet on the ground, put some responsibility on their shoulders.

—Abigail Van Buren
(Dear Abby), advice columnist

What fantastic creatures boys are.

—E. B. White, children's
author, in *Charlotte's Web*

Poverty, race, ethnicity, and immigration status are not in themselves determinative of student achievement. Demography is
not destiny. . . . The court finds that the city's at-risk children
are capable of seizing the opportunity for a sound basic education if they are given sufficient resources.

—Justice Leland DeGrasse,
New York State Supreme Court

Children's talent to endure stems from their ignorance of
alternatives.

—Maya Angelou, writer, educator,
civil rights activist, director, and singer

We should say to each of them [students]: Do you know what
you are? You are a marvel. You are unique . . . there has never
been a child like you. Your legs, your arms, your clever fin-
gers, the way you move. You may become a Shakespeare, a
Michelangelo, a Beethoven. You have the capacity for anything. You are a marvel!

—Pablo Casals, Spanish cellist

I do not think you can ever do enough on behalf of our children.

—Garrison Keillor, public
radio humorist and author

Don't despair a child if he has one clear idea.

—Nathaniel Emmons

"I'm getting dumber every day, and it's all just too embar-
rassing. I'm the only kid in history of education to have a
straight "Z" average!"

—Peppermint Patty in comic
strip *Peanuts*, by Charles Schulz

We worry about what a child will be tomorrow, yet we forget
that he or she is someone today.

—Stacia Tauscher, American educator

The business of being a child interests a child not at all.
Children very rarely play at being other children.

—David Holloway, literary editor

A child miseducated is a child lost.

—John F. Kennedy, U. S. president

Kids don't start at the same place, they don't learn in the same
way, and they don't learn at the same pace.

—Linda Darling-Hammond,
Stanford University, award-winning author

All children wear the sign "I want to be important NOW . . ."

—Dan Pursuit

Childhood is frequently a solemn business to those inside it.

—George Wills, columnist

Children need love especially when they don't deserve it.
—Harold S. Hulbert

You do not merely insert a lot of facts, if you teach them [the students] properly. It is not like injecting 500 cc of serum or administering a year's dose of vitamins.
—Gilbert Highet, author of *The Art of Teaching* (1950)

We should spend less time ranking children and more time helping them to identify their natural competencies and gifts and cultivate these.
—Howard Gardner, Harvard University

Children may forget what you say, but they'll never forget how you make them feel.
—Parker J. Palmer, founder Fetzer Institute,
Teacher Formation Program

I am sure that if people had to choose between living where the noise of children never stopped and where it was never heard, all the good-natured and sound people would prefer incessant noise to incessant silence.
—George Bernard
Shaw, Irish playwright

Every adult needs a child to teach; it's the way adults learn.
—Henry B. Adams, American historian

Here in the city the worst thing that can happen in a nation has happened; we are a people afraid of its youth.
—Elizabeth Hardwick, writer

Children today are tyrants. They contradict their parents, gobble their food, and tyrannize their teachers.

—Socrates, Greek philosopher

Children who are treated as if they are uneducable almost invariably become uneducable.

—Kenneth B. Clark, psychologist,
educator, and social activist

Some kids want to know why teachers get paid when it's the kids who do all the work.

—Milton Berle (Uncle Miltie), comedian

One of the most obvious facts about grown-ups to a child is that they have forgotten what it is like to be a child.

—Randall Jarrell, American author

I'm allergic to spelling.

—Barney Saltzberg, children's author,
in *Phoebe and the Spelling Bee*

You have to watch that word "average." If you have one hand in a fire and the other hand on a block of ice, on the average you're comfortable.

—Les Helm, professor, presenter, and
president of a training and consulting company

Nothing grieves a child more than to study the wrong lesson and learn something he wasn't supposed to.

—E. C. McKenzie, American humorist

What will today's younger generation tell their children they had to do without.

> —Croft M. Pentz, editor of
> *The Complete Book of Zingers*

Nobody can be taught faster than he can learn.

> —Samuel Johnson, British lexicographer and writer

Taxes are important. Just not as important as children.

> —Anonymous spokesperson for Parents United
> for Public Schools, a Minnesota advocacy group

Children usually know the truth before we tell them.

> —Alan Cohen, author

The problems of adolescence have an infinite number of symptoms, but all have the same cause. The cause is preoccupation with self.

> —Linda and Richard Eyre, authors

Right now we have children accountable to the government to pass the tests. What is the government accountable for to the children?

> —Linda Darling-Hammond, Stanford
> University and award-winning author

. . . kids are not political.

> —Jim Rhodes, Minnesota
> House of Representatives

For every student with a spark of brilliance, there are about ten with ignition trouble.

—Milton Berle (Uncle Miltie), comedian

To the best of my knowledge there has been no child in space. I would like to learn about weightlessness, and I'd like to get away from my mother's cooking.

—Jonathan Adashek, age 12, in a letter
to President Ronald Reagan

Most American children suffer from too much mother and too little father.

—Gloria Steinem, American
feminist, writer, and editor

It is the duty of youth to bring its fresh powers to bear on social progress. Each generation of young people should be to the world like a vast reserve force to a tired army. They should lift the world forward. That is what they are for.

—Charlotte P. Gilman, author

Human beings, especially children, are designed to be learning machines. But not all human learning machines are designed for school.

—Aleno Christiano, teacher, teacher
of teachers, lecturer, and writer

I am a Bear of very little Brain, and long words Bother me.

—A. A. Milne, children's
author, in *Winnie-the-Pooh*

By virtually every measure, girls are thriving in school; it is boys who are the second sex.

—Christina Hoff Sommers,
author (*The War Against Boys*, 2001)

What the children become, that will the community become.

—Suzanne LaFollette, author

Our children do not follow our words, but our actions.

—James Baldwin, author

Unlike grown-ups, children have little need to deceive themselves.

—Johann Wolfgang von Goethe,
German writer and scientist

The legacy I want to leave is a child-care system that says no kid is going to be left alone or left behind.

—Marian Wright Edelman, founder
of the Children's Defense Fund

What the hell good is *Brown vs. Board of Education* if no one wants it.

—Bill Cosby, entertainer and
philanthropist, speaking to the
National NAACP convention in 2004

Children have more need of models than of critics.

—Carolyn Coats

Racism is an adult disease. Let's stop spreading it through children.

—Anonymous

Since kids have this huge range of different needs, different interests, and different ways of learning, we've got to have a wide diversity of schools.

—Deborah Meser, educator-author

Kids today are oriented to immediacy. Theirs is a world of fast foods, fast music, fast cars, fast relationships, and fast gratifications. They are not buying our promise for tomorrow because they don't think we can deliver and they are probably right.

—Leroy E. Hay, 1983 National
Teacher of the Year

If Joan of Arc could turn the tide of an entire war before her eighteenth birthday, you can get out of bed.

—Unknown parent to teenager

Handle the children carefully. . . . Remember you're dealing with a sensitive, high-strung little stinker.

—*L and N Magazine*

Teens have a razor-sharp bullshit detector.

—Kenny and Julia Loggins,
musicians and writers

. . . the way students speak to themselves about who they are and how they fit in the world (the voices they listen to in their heads) determines what they do in school.

—William Watson Purkey, author

Never have we exposed children so early and relentlessly to cultural messages glamorizing violence, sex, possessions, alcohol, and tobacco with so few mediating influences from responsible adults. . . . Never have we pushed so many children on to the tumultuous sea of life without the life vests of nurturing families and communities, caring schools, challenged minds, job prospects, and hope.

—Marian Wright Edelman, founder of
the Children's Defense Fund and author

When the commencement speaker told you to "follow your dream," did anyone tell you that you have to wake up first?

—Bill Cosby, entertainer
and philanthropist

Ugh. I hate screaming kids.

—Guy Ritchie, filmmaker,
married to Madonna

All kids need is a little help, a little hope, and somebody who believes in them.

—Ervin "Magic"
Johnson, NBA superstar

What a shame that children are constantly being ranked and evaluated. What a shame it is that superior achievement of one child tends to debase the achievement of another.

—From *Society and the Adolescent Self-Image,*
on the Internet, author unknown

Each Day in America

4 children are killed by abuse or neglect

5 children or teens commit suicide

182 children are arrested for violent crimes

366 children are arrested for drug use

1,186 babies are born to teen mothers

2,171 babies are born in poverty

2,539 high school students drop out

3,742 babies are born to unmarried parents

4,440 children are arrested

17,072 public school students are suspended

—Parent Communication Network
(public school advocacy group)

If you want to be creative, stay in part a child, with the creativity and invention that characterizes children before they are deformed by adult society.

—Jean Piaget, Swiss
developmental psychologist

Nothing you do for a child is ever wasted.

—Garrison Keillor, public
radio humorist and author

We must all work to make the world worthy of its children.

—Pablo Casals, Spanish cellist

Apply yourself. Get all the education you can, but then do something. Don't just stand there, make it happen.

—Lee Iacocca, business magnate
(CEO Chrysler Corporation) and
TV commercial actor

We have few contemporary heroes but we have plenty of trash-talking, high-flying, stuff-strutting celebrities who seem transfixed by their own images. Is it any wonder that youngsters disrespect authority. They've learned well from the "heroes" who only watch out for number one.

—Richard G. Copen, Sr., author

Kids! What on earth's the matter with kids today? Kids! Always rude, obnoxious, and in the way! Why can't they be more like us? Perfect in every way. What's the matter with kids today?

—from the Broadway
musical *Bye Bye Birdie*

You can do anything with children if you only play with them.

—Prince Otto von Bismarck,
German statesman

There had always been kids in school who were smart—that is the school said they were smart, they could be shown to have been smart at some time in their own lives on the school's own tests—but who did not do well in school, who got bad grades, and who were a pain in the ass.

—James Iteindon, author

⟮◦⟯

They [the students] make me feel alive and let me live again as a 12-year-old. Their passion for learning is inspiring.

—Nouchie Xiong, 18, intern in the Breakthrough St. Paul program for students exploring a career in teaching

⟮◦⟯

The responsibility to make choices and to institute change is the child's.

—Virginia M. Axline

⟮◦⟯

We pray for children . . . who never get dessert, who watch their parents watch them die, who can't find any bread to steal, who don't have any room to clean, whose pictures aren't on anybody's dresser, whose monsters are real. . . .

We pray for children who want to be carried and for those who must, for those we never give up on and for those who don't get a second chance.

For those we smother . . . and for those who will grab the hand of anybody kind enough to offer it.

—excerpts from a
prayer by Ina J. Hughes

⟮◦⟯

Teachers have two sets of children to deal with. One set of kids have a parent who listens to them read . . . and instills the value of education. . . . The other set of kids have parents who care but who cannot or do not do the parenting job well because they are crippled by their own confusion.

—Jim Klimmek, fifth-grade teacher, Hayden
Heights Elementary School, St. Paul, Minnesota

Don't limit a child to your own learning, for he was born to another time.

—Rabbinical saying

If school results were the key to power, girls would be running the world.

—Sarah Boseley

About what's wrong with grown-ups . . . is that they think they know all the answers.

—Zilpha Keatley Snyder,
children's author (*The Changeling*)

The thing that impresses me most about America is the way parents obey their children.

—Duke of Windsor, 1967

Let your children grow tall and some taller than others if they have it in them to do so.

—Margaret Thatcher,
British prime minister

Children are unpredictable. You never know what inconsistencies they're going to catch you in next.

—Franklin P. Jones,
humorist and writer

No matter where you hide your sex magazines, your teenager will find them.

—Bruce Lansky, writer

We must have a place where children can have a whole group of adults they can trust.

—Margaret Mead, anthropologist

Normal adolescent is sometimes very abnormal.

—Leigh Abrahamson, school social worker

A child should not be denied a balloon because an adult knows that sooner or later it will burst.

—Marcelion Cox, American author

You can learn many things from children. How much patience you have for instance.

—Franklin P. Jones, humorist and writer

Children are the keys to paradise.

—Richard Henry
Stoddard, poet and critic

Every child is an artist. The problem is how to remain an artist when we grow up.

—Pablo Picasso, painter

No one ever kept a secret better than a child.
—Victor Hugo, French author

Every generation rebels against its fathers and makes friends with its grandfathers.
—Lewis Mumford, writer

The greatest terror a child can have is that he is not loved, and rejection is the hell he fears.
—John Steinbeck,
American novelist

Never help a child with a task at which he feels he can succeed.
—Maria Montessori, early childhood
education innovator, founder of
Montessori schools worldwide

We ought to be doing all we can to make it possible for every child to fulfill his or her God-given potential.
—Hillary Rodham Clinton,
U. S. senator and former first lady

The future of America walks through the doors of our schools every day.
—Mary Jean LeTendre

The teachers' working conditions are the students' learning conditions.
—Moulthrup, Calegarie, and Eggers,
authors of *Teachers Have It Easy*

Children are the living messages we send to a time we will not see.

—Attributed to Neil Postman and to
John W. Whitehead, authors

Each student brings something different to the table to add to a diverse collaboration of ideas, thoughts, and knowledge.

—Lunsine Toure, 27, intern
in the Breakthrough St. Paul program for
students exploring a career in teaching

Children are on two trains, one heading to bad ends and one to good ends. What we need are more switching stations.

—Attributed to Carl Holmstrom, former
superintendent of schools, St. Louis Park, Minnesota

Children may be 20 percent of the population, but they are 100 percent of the future.

—David B. Tyack, Stanford University

Teaching

Is teaching an art or a science? Yes. And more! What teachers do every day doesn't seem too remarkable until you try it.

One day in the classroom would be enough to convince most people that teaching is not only the greatest profession, but the toughest and most complicated as well.

Following are some of the best things anybody ever said about this remarkable process and profession called teaching.

Every morning, hundreds of thousands of adults handle the most demanding audience anyone could ever hope to know—a roomful of students—in what many would argue is the most important job in our society: teaching.

—From the flyleaf of *The Quotable Teacher*, edited by Randy Howe

I feel as though teaching is 10 percent inspiration and 90 percent divine call.

—Susan Soares, teacher, Bristol, Rhode Island

What nobler employment, or more valuable to the state, than that of the man who instructs the next generation.

—Cicero, Roman statesman, orator, and philosopher

Teaching is the greatest act of optimism.

—Colleen Wilcox

When the uncapped potential of a student meets the liberating art of a teacher, a miracle unfolds.

—Mary Hatwood Futrell, college dean and president of education international

I was still learning when I taught my last class.

—Claude M. Fuess, American educator

Teaching is like a wild and crazy rafting adventure on mega challenging terrain . . . exhilarating, exciting, strenuous, exhausting, rewarding, and unpredictable, very up and down. One minute you are laughing and smiling, the next crying. But it's a rafting adventure for the huge cause of making a difference in the lives of others.

—Unnamed teacher quoted in *Creating a Positive Culture* by Marie-Nathalie Beaudoin and Maureen Taylor

Training is everything: the peach was once a bitter almond; cauliflower is nothing but cabbage with a college education.
—Mark Twain, humorist and author

Let how you live your life stand for something, no matter how small and incidental it may seem.
—Jodie Foster, Oscar-winning actress and director

. . . the greatest gifts that a teacher can give to a student: confidence and passion.
—Alec Baldwin, actor

. . . when he [the teacher] goes into the classroom, shuts the door, takes the lonely seat behind the desk and looks into the shining morning faces, then he is thrown back absolutely on himself. No power on earth can help him, and nothing can save the situation if he makes a blunder.
—William Lyon Phelps

Teaching children to count is not as important as teaching them what counts.
Arlene Greco, Christian author

Technology is just a tool. In terms of getting the kids working together and motivating them, the teacher is the most important.
—Bill Gates, billionaire computer industry magnate, Microsoft cofounder

A teacher who is attempting to teach without inspiring the pupil with a desire to learn is hammering on a cold iron.

—Horace Mann, educator and politician

I cannot teach anybody anything; I can only make them think.

—Socrates, Greek philosopher and teacher

To know how to suggest is the art of teaching.

—Henri Frederic Amiel,
Swiss philosopher and writer

The educator must above all understand how to wait; to reckon all effects in the light of the future, not the present.

—Ellen Key, Swedish author

It's all to do with training; you can do a lot if you're properly trained.

—Queen Elizabeth II

The answers aren't important really . . . what's important is—knowing all the questions.

—Zilpha Keatley Snyder,
children's author, in *The Changeling*

Love truth, but pardon error.

—Voltaire, Enlightenment
philosopher and author

Describing her first day back in grade school after a long absence, a teacher said, "It was like trying to hold thirty-five corks under water at the same time."

—Mark Twain, humorist and author

Everything I learn about teaching I learn from bad students.

—John Holt, educator

The sound that best describes teaching is the sound of a car being driven by someone just learning how to drive a stick shift. It's getting somewhere, but nowhere quickly, and there are a lot of stops and starts in between.

—Margaret Stuhar, English teacher

A child cannot be taught by anyone who despises them. . . .

—James Baldwin, African American
expatriate, author, and preacher

The best teachers give their pupils both a sense of order, discipline, control; and a powerful stimulus which urges them to take their destinies in their own hands, kick over rules, and transgress all boundaries.

—Gilbert Highet, professor-author

What I live, I impart.

—Augustine, Catholic Saint

To be sure there is an age-old prejudice against teaching.

—Jacques Barzun,
French-born American educator

And half the fun of nearly everything, you know, is thinking about it beforehand, or afterward.

—Howard R. Garis, children's author,
in *Uncle Wiggly's Storybook*

To teach is not to transfer knowledge but to create the possibilities for the production or construction of knowledge.

—Paulo Freire, Brazilian educationalist

The only reason I always try to meet and know the parents better is because it helps me to forgive their children.

—Louis Johannot, educator

The object of teaching a child is to enable him to get along without his teacher.

—Elbert Hubbard, author-publisher

Teaching is truth mediated by personality.

—Phyllis Brooks

It is . . . sometimes easier to head an institute for the study of child guidance than it is to turn one brat into a decent human being.

—Joseph Wood
Krutch, essayist and teacher

It is no matter what you teach first, any more than what leg you shall put into your breeches first.

—Samuel Johnson,
British lexicographer

Just think of the tragedy of teaching children not to doubt.
—Clarence Darrow, attorney

... it is memorable students rather than professional mile-
stones that highlight the phases of a typical career in teaching.
—Susan Mone Johnson, Howard University

There's nothing so unequal as the equal treatment of unequals.
—Anonymous

To me the sole hope of human salvation lies in teaching.
—George Bernard Shaw, Irish dramatist

Teaching is painful, continual, and difficult work to be done
by kindness . . . and by praise, but above all by example.
—John Ruskin, British author and art critic

A Teacher's Lament

It is already August. It blows my mind.
Soon we'll be back to the same old grind.

Of putting up bulletin boards, papers and such—
Who knew that teaching would require so much.

Yet as we walk into September's class,
Eager eyes and smiles will make time pass.

We'll listen, we'll nurture, we'll love each voice
And know after all—we made the right choice.
—Linda Peterson, educator

Guide them [children] as they grow, show them in every way, that they are cared for, and make special moments for them that will add magic to their lives; motivate them to make a difference in the life of others; and, most important, teach them to love life.

—Ron Clark, Disney
Teacher of the Year, 2001

. . . Teaching is brain surgery without breaking the skin.

—Daniel Walker, former
Alaska Teacher of the Year

Remember, Custer had a plan.

—Noah ben Shea, poet, lecturer,
philosopher, and best-selling author

Practice is the best of all instructors.

—Publilius Syrus, writer

If I were asked to enumerate the educational stupidities, the giving of grades would head the list . . . if I can't give a child a better reason for studying than studying for a grade on a report card, I ought to lock my desk and go home and stay there.

—Dorothy DeZouche, educator

To say that you have taught when students haven't learned is to say you have sold when no one has bought.

—Madeline Hunter, educator,
author, and teacher trainer

Children need all school workers. A person is not "just a jani-tor," not "just a custodian," they're partners in education. We need each other to make this work.

—Rev. Jesse Jackson, political and civil rights activist

Tell me and I'll forget. Show me and I may not remember. Involve me and I'll understand.

—Native American saying

Schools cannot shut their door and expect a "safe castle" where outside influences don't enter.

—Carl Bosch, German industrial chemist

We teach what we like to learn and the reason many people go into teaching is vicariously to re-experience the primary joy experienced the first time they learned something they loved.

—Stephen Brookfield, educator

We are fortunate to work in a noble and honorable profession where we have the power, the ability, and the compassion nec-essary to make the world a better place.

—John Blaydes, educator,
author, and motivational speaker

To teach is to transform by informing, to develop a zest for lifelong learning, to help pupils become students—mature independent learners, architects of an exciting, challenging future. Teaching at its best is a kind of communion, a meeting and a merging of mind.

—Edgar Dale, educator-author,
readability formula expert

Education should be gentle and stern, not cold and lax.
> —Joseph Joubert, musical
> accompanist, director, arranger,
> producer, and orchestrator

c❦

I'm bilingual. I speak English and educationese.
> —Shirley Hufstedler, U. S. congresswoman
> and U. S. secretary of education

c❦

Nothing has better effect on children than praise.
> —Sir Philip Sidney, English
> poet and writer

c❦

The ideal committee is one with me as chairman and two other members in bed with the flu.
> —Lord Milverton

c❦

Teaching is the world's most important job.
> —UNESCO publication

c❦

Teaching is the real world—it's like making love standing up in a hammock—you need balance, grace, and a hell of a lot of perseverance.
> —Hanoch McCarty,
> motivational speaker and writer

c❦

Good teaching is one-fourth preparation and three-fourths theater.
> —Gail Godwin, novelist

c❦

Any genuine teaching will result, if successful, in someone's knowing how to bring about a better condition of things than existed before.

—John Dewey, educator and philosopher

No other job in the world could possibly dispossess one so completely as this job of teaching. You could stand all day in a laundry, for instance, still in possession of your mind. But this teaching utterly obliterates you. It cuts right into your being; essentially, it takes over your spirit.

—Sylvia Ashton-Warner, educator-writer

The secret of teaching is to appear to have known all your life what you learned this afternoon.

—Anonymous

Labels belong on cans, not people.

—Vicki Caruana, curriculum designer and writer

It's [teaching] kind of like having a love affair with a rhinoceros.

—Anne Sexton, poet and writer

I'll never learn to spell. The teachers keep changing the words.

—Henny Youngman, comedian

The vanity of teaching doth oft tempt a man to forget that he is a blockhead.

—George Savile, Marques de Halifax

Don't find fault. Find a remedy.

—Henry Ford, father of the
American automobile industry

⸙

To teach, to guide, to explain, to help, to nurture—these are life's noblest attainments.

—Frank Tyger

⸙

The work that the schoolmaster is doing is inestimable in its consequences.

—Stephen Leacock, Canadian
columnist and humorous writer

⸙

Good teaching is more a giving of right questions than giving of right answers.

—Josef Albers, artist and teacher

⸙

The one exclusive sign of thorough knowledge is the power of teaching.

—Aristotle, Greek philosopher

⸙

First, teach a person to develop to the point of his limitations and then—pfft!—break the limitations.

—Viola Spolin, creator of improv

⸙

If you tell a child enough times that they are smart and that they can do something, they start to believe they can.

—Carolyn McCarthy, nurse, housewife, gun
violence opponent, and U. S. congresswoman

⸙

The teacher's art consists in this: To turn the child's attention from trivial details and to guide his thoughts continually towards relations of importance which he will one day need to know that he may judge rightly of good and evil in society.
—Jean-Jacques Rousseau,
French philosopher

How to be a good teacher: Teach the basic subject. Have an atmosphere conducive to learning. Hold the students accountable for progress. Have performance standards.
—Colonel Patrick Harrington,
United States Marine Corps

Teach us delight in simple things . . .
—Rudyard Kipling, author and poet

Teaching is the royal road to learning.
—Jessamyn West, author

You could work as many hours as you want. You would never find an end to your time. Even when I go places and do activities with my family, I see [everything] as a teacher. I'm always thinking, "What can I use? This would be neat."
—Unnamed fifth-grade teacher quoted in
Creating a Positive School Culture, by
Marie-Nathalie Beaudoin and Maureen Taylor

Make your classroom a safe place to dream.
—Vicki Caruana, curriculum
designer and author

It is the supreme art of the teacher to awaken joy in creative expression and knowledge.

—Albert Einstein, physicist

Teaching is what I want to do with my life.

The task of the teacher is to balance the difficult juggling act of becoming vitally, vigorously, creatively, energetically, and inspiringly unnecessary.

—Gerald O. Grow, educator

Trust, not submission, defines obedience.

—Joan W. Bios, children's author (*A Gathering of Days*)

Teach today; be remembered tomorrow.

—Vicki Caruana, curriculum designer and author

In teaching, it is the drawing out, not the pumping in.

—Ashley Montagu, anthropologist

The art of teaching is the art of assisting discovery.

—Mark Van Doren, poet, writer, and critic

Teaching is as interesting as teachers make it.

—Becky Goodwin, former Kansas Teacher of the Year

Teaching is what I want to do with my life.

—Unnamed social studies teacher
in an inner-city school

We expect teachers to handle teenage pregnancy, substance abuse, and the failings of the family. Then we expect them to educate our children.

—John Sculley, businessman

Your methods are like slow-release fertilizer; over time they produce a bountiful harvest.

—Vicki Caruana, curriculum designer and author

We must teach our children to dream with their eyes open.

—Harry Edwards, American sociologist

There are always more events to be organized, students to be congratulated, cheers to say, homework to design, and challenges to meet.

—Pondie Nicholson, 21, intern in the Breakthrough St. Paul program for students exploring a career in teaching

We have a real problem. We need to start treating teachers as professionals in how we train them, how we pay them, and how we treat them in a professional setting.

—Tim Pawlenty, Minnesota governor, speaking to the Minnesota Business Partnership, September 8, 2004

A pint of example is worth a gallon of advice.

—Unknown

If I had a child who wanted to be a teacher, I would bid him Godspeed as if he were going to war.

—James Hilton, British novelist

Good teaching is an art, and can neither be defined nor standardized.

—Joel H. Hildebrand,
Berkeley University professor,
approaching his 101st birthday

If we don't model what we teach, we are teaching something else.

—Abraham Maslow,
psychologist specializing
in higher-level thinking skills

Teach so that what is offered is perceived as a valuable gift and not a hard duty.

Vicki Caruana,
curriculum designer and author

Never try to teach a pig to sing. You'll waste your time and it annoys the pig.

—Les Helm, professor,
presenter, and president of a
training and consulting company

There are few jobs as demanding as teaching: minute to minute, hour to hour—at all times, a teacher has to be on.

—Dave Eggers, Daniel Moulthrop, and
Ninive Clements Calegari,
authors of *Teachers Have It Easy*

Those of us who work in the field of education are neither bank tellers who have little discretion nor assembly line workers whose actions are largely repetitive. Each child we teach is wonderfully unique, and each requires us to use in our work that most exquisite of human capacities, the ability to make judgments in the absence of rules.

—Eliot W. Eisner, professor of
education and art, Stanford University

No one rises to low expectations.

—Rev. Jesse Jackson, political and
civil rights activist

Teach to the problems, not to the text.

—E. K. M. Nebeuts

Example isn't another way to teach, it is the only way to teach.

—Albert Einstein, physicist

The task of the modern educator is not to cut jungles, but to irrigate ditches.

—C. S. Lewis, British
writer and critic

A master can tell you what he expects of you. A teacher, though, awakens your own expectations.

—Unknown

Decide today to be a tiller in your classroom.

—Vicki Caruana, curriculum
designer and author

If you have an important point to make, don't try to be subtle or clever. Use a pile driver. Hit the point once. Then come back and hit it again. Then hit it a third time—a tremendous whack.
—Sir Winston Churchill,
British prime minister in World War II,
speaker, author, and historian

Teaching is the hardest work I had ever done, and it remains the hardest work I have done to date.
—Ann Richards, former
governor of Texas

Teaching is the greatest act of wisdom.
—Colleen Wilcox, writer

Teach these things and make sure everyone learns them well . . . be their ideal; let me follow the way you teach and live.
—The Bible, 1 Timothy, 4:11–12

If you do not actually like boys and girls, or young men and women, give up teaching.
—Gilbert Highet, *The Art of Teaching*,
Scottish-born American classicist

The whole secret of the teacher's force lies in the conviction that men are convertible.
—Ralph Waldo Emerson, author, minister,
founder of American transcendentalism

Segregation was wrong when it was forced by white people, and I believe it is still wrong when it is requested by black people.

—Coretta Scott King, civil rights activist,
widow of Martin Luther King

A professional is someone who can do his best work when he doesn't feel like it.

—Alfred Alistair Cook,
journalist and broadcaster

The real menace in dealing with a 5-year-old is that in no time, you begin to sound like a 5-year-old.

—Jean Kerv, author, humorist

I worry about the future of education as veteran teachers retire; we must cultivate the dignity and emphasize the societal worth of the individual teacher and the teaching profession.

—Barbara Gordon, former
New York Teacher of the Year

I have found nothing more toxic to a healthy learning environment than an overdose of constant criticism.

Roland S. Barth, education consultant, author,
founder of Harvard Principal Center, and avid sailor

The mind is more vulnerable than the stomach, because it can be poisoned without feeling immediate pain.

—Helen MacInnes, spy novelist

Fifty years ago teachers said their top discipline problems were talking, chewing gum, making noise, and running in the halls. The current list, by contrast, sounds like a cross between a rap sheet and the seven deadly sins.

—Anne Quindlen, author

. . . the true heroes of our society are not found on a movie screen or football field. They are to be found in our classrooms.

—Elizabeth Dole, U. S. senator

What office is there which involves more responsibility, which requires more qualifications, and which ought, therefore, to be more honorable, than that of teaching?

—Harriet Martineau, English writer

Socrates didn't have an overhead projector. He asked questions that bothered people and 3,500 years later people are still talking about him.

—Hanoch McCarty, speaker and writer

Of course class size is important! You have to find the child to teach the child.

—Unknown

It has long been clear to me that teaching is the most difficult and the most honorable of professions.

—William Friday, author

Teaching is a wonderful profession for those who love to learn because there is always something new happening or a new way to look at something you have been doing.

—Alene Christiano, teacher, teacher of
teachers, lecturer, and author

To know that even one life has breathed easier because you have lived, this is to have succeeded.

—Ralph Waldo Emerson, author, minister,
founder of American transcendentalism

Homework is a breeze. Cooking is a pleasant diversion. Putting up a retaining wall is a lark. But teaching is like climbing a mountain.

—Fawn M. Brodie, author

Generally speaking, the more we try to improve our schools, the heavier the teacher's task becomes and the better our teaching methods, the more difficult they are to apply.

—Jean Piaget, Swiss developmental psychologist

For every time we drop our standards, hold our nose, and hire any adult who can fog a mirror, we run the risk of placing a mistake in the classroom for thirty years.

—Kati Haycock, director of the Education Trust

It seems like there's very little appreciation for people in our society who work with kids. I just keep wondering, when is it that teachers became the bad guys?

—Bonnie Rosenfield,
former Minneapolis teacher

Teaching is the best way I know of regaining balance in your egocentric outlook on life.

> —Barbara Gaspavik,
> child development teacher

Unfortunately, teaching is often times like golf, so many bad shots in between the good. And those are the few shots that we need to remember.

> —Howard Nereo, fifth-grade
> teacher, New Haven, Connecticut

My heart is singing for joy this morning. A miracle has happened! The light of understanding has shone upon my little pupil's mind—and, behold, all things are changed.

> —Annie Sullivan, Helen Keller's teacher

Teaching is instructing, advising, counseling, organizing, assessing, guiding, goading, showing, managing, modeling, coaching, disciplining, prodding, preaching, persuading, proselytizing, listening, interacting, nursing, and inspiring

> —Gloria Ladson-Billings,
> University of Wisconsin

Good teaching cannot be reduced to technique; good teaching comes from the identity and integrity of the teacher.

> —Parker J. Palmer, founder, Fetzer
> Institute Teacher Formation Program

I like a teacher who gives you something to take home to think about besides homework.

> —Lily Tomlin, comedian

Let early education be a sort of amusement; you will then be better able to find out the natural bent.

—Plato, Greek philosopher

Let early education be a sort of amusement; you will then be better able to find out the natural bent.

The dream begins with a teacher who believes in you, who tugs and pushes and leads you to the next plateau, sometimes poking you with a sharp stick called truth.

—Dan Rather, TV news reporter and anchorman

To teach is to learn.

—Japanese proverb

There is a much more sensible approach to improving education . . . that is to produce a cohort of teachers who believe they are professional, who act like professionals, and who are treated as professionals.

—Howard Gardner, Harvard University

There is no higher religion than human service. To work for the common good is the greatest creed.

—Albert Schweitzer,
Nobel Peace Prize–winning
philosopher, musician, theologian,
physician, and humanitarian

Powerful people take the jobs that entrust them with the important things. If you want good people in the teaching profession, you have to set it up so teachers have authority over the important things.

—Theodore Sizer, founder,
Coalition of Essential Schools

A life of teaching is a stitched-together affair, a crazy quilt of odd pieces and scrounged materials, equal parts invention and imposition.

—Gloria Ladson-Billings,
University of Wisconsin

Rules for Teachers—1915

1. You will not marry during the term of your contract.

2. You are not to keep company with men.

3. You must be home between the hours of 8 P.M. and 6 A.M. unless attending a school function.

4. You may not loiter downtown at ice cream shops. . . .

5. You must under no circumstances dye your hair.

6. You must wear at least two petticoats.

—Source: Cabell County, West
Virginia, Board of Education, Old
Sacramento Schoolhouse Museum

As you well know, there are few professions as challenging as teaching . . . the increasing complexity of the world, with burdensome social issues and shifting economic demands makes the work more difficult than ever before. Yet, for those like you who choose the profession and dedicate yourself to doing it well, the rewards make the journey worthwhile.

—Peter McWalters, Rhode Island
state commissioner of education

Never threaten a child: either punish him or forgive him. . . . If you must strike a child, use a string.

—The Talmud

The greatest satisfactions of . . . teaching are not found in pay, prestige, or promotion, but in psychic rewards.

—Michael Fullan, educator-author

A young teacher, returning to college to hone her skills, asks herself why she wants to teach children who do not have a safe environment to learn in and who lack resources and support from administrators and family. Besides her intrinsic love for teaching, we need to give her a reason to stay.

—Bill Cosby, entertainer and philanthropist

Do you know another business or profession where highly skilled specialists are required to tally numbers, alphabetize cards, put notices in mailboxes, and patrol the lunchroom?

—Bel Kaufman, German-born American novelist, and New York City teacher for 20 years

The key to everything is patience. You get the chicken by hatching the egg—not by smashing it.

—Ellen Glasgow, novelist

There is nothing more inspiring than having a mind unfold before you. Let people teach who have a calling. It is never just a job.

—Abraham Kaplan, philosopher, author, and educator

If a doctor, lawyer, or dentist had 40 people in their office at one time, all of whom had different needs, and some of whom didn't want to be there and were causing trouble, and the doctor, lawyer, or dentist, without assistance, had to treat all

with professional excellence for nine months, then he might have some conception of the classroom teacher's job.
—Donald D. Quitin, author

౸౸

Teaching is basically "an imaginative act of hope."
—William Watson Parker,
author of *What Students Say to Themselves*

౸౸

Upon our children—how they are taught—rest the fate—or future—of tomorrow's world.
—B. C. Forbes, founder, *Forbes* magazine

౸౸

School leaders must never forget that teaching is the real business of schools.
—Leonard Pellicer, dean of School of Education
and Organizational Leadership, University of La Vern

౸౸

If teaching our young in schools becomes a lifelong professional career—adequately rewarded and supported; with decision-making authority commensurate with responsibilities—teacher shortages would fade away.
—John I. Goodlad, Center of Educational
Research, University of Washington

౸౸

When teachers have a low expectation for their children's learning, the children seldom exceed their expectation. This is a self-fulfilling prophecy.
—John Niemeyer

౸౸

In education, surprise ought to be seen not as a limitation but as the mark of creative work. Surprise breeds freshness and discovery.

—Elliot W. Eisner, Stanford University

Teaching tugs at the heart, opens the heart, even breaks the heart—and the more one loves teaching, the more heartbreaking it can be. The courage to teach is the courage to keep one's heart open in those very moments when the heart is asked to hold more than it is able so that teacher and students and subject can be woven into the fabric of community that teaching and learning requires.

—Parker J. Palmer, founder, Fetzer Institute Teacher Formation Program

The mind is like the stomach. It is not how much you put into it that counts, but how much it digests.

—Albert Jay Nock, author, educator, and social critic

The greatest gift is the passion for reading. It is cheap, it consoles, it distracts, it excites, it gives you knowledge of the world experience of a wide kind.

—Elizabeth Hardwick, author

The Teachers Lament

You know you've been teaching too long when:

- You take attendance everywhere you go.
- Your bladder works only at 50-minute intervals.
- You can't do anything without a form.

- You really look forward to meetings.
- You eat all your meals in less than 15 minutes. . . .

—Jeanne Quamme

Teaching is not always about passing on what you know; it is passing on who you are.

—Kenny and Julia Loggins,
musicians and writers

The volume of paperwork expands to fill the available briefcase.

—Jerry Brown, former
governor of California

Never tell people how to do things. Tell them what to do and they will surprise you with their ingenuity.

—General George S. Patton,
U. S. military leader in World War II

Quality schoolwork . . . can only be achieved in a warm, supportive classroom environment. It cannot exist if there is an adversarial relationship. . . . Above all, there must be trust.

—William Glasser, founder, William Glasser Institute

You can't fatten the cattle by weighing them—you have to feed them.

—Paul D. Houston, executive director of the
American Association of School Administrators,
speaking about executive training

Spring weather is very seductive . . . we've got to modify the way we teach to accommodate what the children are thinking of and longing to do.

—Sylvia Seidel, educator

Imparting knowledge is only lighting other men's candles at our lamp, without depriving ourselves of any flame.

—Jane Porter, author

In the education of children there is nothing like alluring the interest and affection, otherwise, you only make so many asses laden with books.

—Michel Eyquem de
Montaigne, French essayist

Brilliance depends on who's writing the test.

—Garrison Keillor, public radio
personality, author, and humorist

When you're a teacher, you've got to have something they call "with-it-ness." You have to be on top of everything, have eyes in the back of your head.

—Kelly Maynard, middle school
teacher and former journalist

Teaching in schools is too often a system of tension disguised as learning.

—Noah ben Shea, poet, lecturer,
philosopher, and best-selling writer

I believe in second chances, so I don't give up on people or children. I know that if I have a class full of kids, I want them all to succeed. . . . I am going to give my students as many chances as they need to find themselves as students.

—Ennis Cosby, teacher (deceased son of Bill Cosby)

Who is going to teach tomorrow's children? The answer to this question is a major concern confronting policymakers as they face teacher shortages and search for ways to improve education.

—Sylvia Mei-ling, researcher and
teacher, Teachers College, Columbia University

Plan lessons that give the mind a chance to do the job it is intended to do. The mind's jobs are to use what is known to meet challenges, to use what is known to make discoveries, and . . . to use what is known to create new knowing.

—Alene Christiano, teacher, teacher
of teachers, lecturer, and writer

Kids are fun people in general. Adults have learned to be adults . . . and kids haven't learned that yet. They just live right through their skin and I can be more that way because I'm with them all the time. I don't have to put myself in this adult shell all the time, and I can be weird and funny and dance and they love it.

—Maggie Knutson, fifth-grade teacher
(recipient of a $25,000 award from
the Milken Family Foundation)

You can't teach good character, if you don't have it.

—Tim Lickona, psychologist and educator

If there is nothing else that we model to our students, I think we need to model that moment of ambiguity: that ability to leave questions unanswered, that ability to listen to opposing views without choosing a side, that ability to speak passionately about one's position while acknowledging that perhaps, somewhere down the line, that position might change. When we model this, we can provide a place where students can feel encouraged to speak and even engage in conflict without simultaneously feeling that each conflict will have a winner or loser.

—Phyllis M. Ryder, educator

The first and great commandment is, don't let them scare you.

—Elmer Davis

We upped our test scores—up yours.

—Bumper sticker on a teacher's car

A tennis shoe in a laundry dryer. Probably no image captures as fully the life of an adult working in an elementary, middle, or senior high school. For educators, schoolwork much of the time is turbulent, heated, confused, disoriented, congested, and full of recurring bumps.

—Roland S. Barth, educational consultant, founder of Harvard Principal Center, and avid sailor

Our problem as educators is that far too often we begin the academic year worrying more about our courses . . . than about our students, those fragile human beings who sit across from us and stare waiting to learn and eager to know.

—Frank Pajares, educator

There's no trick to coaching. If the team had a good game, they did it. If they had an average game, we did it. If they have a bad game, it's my fault. That's all you need to know about coaching.

—Bear Bryant, legendary football
coach at the University of Alabama

Spoon-feeding in the long run teaches us nothing but the shape of the spoon

—E. M. Forster, author

The teacher should never lose his temper in the presence of the class. If a man, he may take refuge in profane soliloquies; if a woman, she may follow the example of one sweet-faced and apparently tranquil girl—go out in the yard and gnaw a post.

—William Lyon Phelps, American educator

The rewards of teaching come from teachers' innate belief that every day they have the opportunity to enrich the lives of their students by igniting the human spirit, dignifying the human experience, and inspiring human excellence.

—John Blaydes, educator, author, and motivational speaker

It is a greater work to educate a child, in the true and logical sense of the world, than to rule a state.

—William Ellery Channing, American minister

Popular culture has long celebrated other heroes—the athlete, the adventurer, the statesman . . . teachers have not been cele-brated in the same way. And classrooms have rarely been identified as the place where the greatest of human drama unfolds—the drama of igniting the human spirit, enabling the human art, and enriching the human experience.

—IBM TV commercial

Teaching is not a lost art, but the regard for it is a lost tradition.

—Jacques Barzun, French-born
American educator

A wealthy CEO expounded to everyone in sight about his high salary, hefty bonuses, and liberal stock options. Then, he asked a young teacher, "And what do you make?" The teacher replied, "I make kids work harder than they thought they could. I make them question—criticize—write—read—I make them understand that if you have the brains, then follow your heart. You know what I make? I make a difference."

—Thomas L. Friedman, Pulitzer
Prize–winning columnist and author

There is no job that requires professionals more than teaching, yet there is no job in which the people who do it are treated in ways that make it impossible for them to be professional. Imagine what medicine or law would be like if physicians and lawyers were treated as teachers are.

—William Glasser, founder,
William Glasser Institute

. . . teachers love their jobs because teaching can be the most emotionally rewarding, intellectually invigorating, and soul-satisfying job on earth.

— Dave Eggers, Daniel Moulthrop, and
Ninive Clements Calegari, authors of *Teachers Have It Easy*

... one of teaching's great rewards is the daily chance it gives us to get back to the dance floor. It is the dance of the spiraling generations in which the old empower the young with their experience and the young empower the old with new life, reweaving the fabric of the human community as they touch and turn.

—Parker J. Palmer, founder,
Fetzer Institute Teacher Formation Program

No calling in society is more demanding than teaching, no calling in our society is more selfless than teaching, and no calling is more central to the vitality of a democracy than teaching.

—Roger Mudd, news reporter
and commentator

Teachers

George Bernard Shaw once said that only those who can do nothing else become teachers. Shaw was wrong.

Although there may be a few losers or rejects who somehow manage to take up space in the classroom until a real teacher comes along, the truth is that the men and women who make good teachers can do almost anything, but choose to teach. In fact, effective teachers have to be masters of many trades. Teachers invented "multitasking" long before it became popular.

Walk in the shoes of a teacher—any teacher—and you will quickly discover that teaching is no profession for sissies, slackers, charlatans, pretenders, wannabes, or also-rans. It is a tough business for tough, talented, tenacious professionals.

Many are called to teaching (some for the wrong reasons—e.g., summers off). But few are chosen to stay the course as lifelong educators. If you are one of the few who can teach well, why would you do anything else?

Is it just me? Or are teachers very special people engaged in America's greatest profession? For answers, look at what others say about society's everyday classroom heroes.

No bubble is so iridescent or floats longer than that blown by the successful teacher.

—Sir William Osler, Canadian physician

A gifted teacher is as rare as a gifted doctor.

—Anonymous

As a teacher, I have to be a symphony conductor. Sometimes the brass is too brash and the percussion is too loud. I sense the tempo and mood and alter it if necessary.

—Unnamed teacher quoted in *Creating a Positive School Culture* by Marie-Nathalie Beaudoin and Maureen Taylor

A school teacher handles many more children than a parent, and is given two months vacation every year to recuperate.

—Evan Esar, humorist

When you are a teacher you are always in the right place at the right time. There is no wrong time for learning . . . any time a student is there before you, the possibility is present, the moment is yours.

—Betty B. Anderson

A teacher affects eternity; he can never tell where his influence stops.

—Henry B. Adams,
historian-journalist

I do not teach children, I give them joy.

—Isadora Duncan, legendary dancer

Teachers have always been creative just as the world has always been round.
—Randy Howe, special education
teacher and author

The most extraordinary thing about a really good teacher . . . is that he or she transcends accepted educational methods.
—Margaret Mead, anthropologist and author

. . . We will be teaching, loving, and guiding all the kids, regardless of color, every hour, every day, every year, because we know we are the only chance some kids have.
—Jeff Klimmek, fifth-grade teacher, Hayden
Heights Elementary School, St. Paul, Minnesota

Teachers, I believe, are the most responsible and important members of society because their professional efforts affect the fate of the earth.
—Helen Caldicott, Australian physician,
author, professor, and peace activist

The word "teacher" encompasses great responsibility and even greater rewards.
—Mary Rodarte, author-educator

Good teachers empathize with kids, respect them, and believe that each one has something special that can be built upon.
—Ann Lieberman, professor
emerita, columbia University

Question: If I became a great teacher, who would ever know?

Response: You, your students, and God. Not a bad audience.
—from the movie, *A Man For All Seasons*

Teachers usually have no way of knowing that they have made a difference in a child's life, even when they have made a dramatic one. . . . Good teachers put snags in the river of children passing by, and over the years, they redirect hundreds of lives.

—Tracy Kidder, Pulitzer Prize–winning author

They do everything but leap tall buildings for their students. Their super hearing detects questions before they're even asked. They pluck kids from short attention spans and awe them with new discoveries. Their keen vision sees potential where others can't. While it may be hard to recognize teachers on the street, it's easy to recognize the results of their work in the classroom.

—Promotional ad for Education Minnesota
(teacher union affiliated with both NEA and AFT)

Joey is the mouth. There is one in every class along with the complainer, the clown, the goody-goody, the beauty queen, the volunteer for everything, the jock, the intellectual, the momma's boy, the mystic, the sissy, the lover, the critic, the jerk, the religious fanatic who sees sin everywhere, the brooding one who sits in the back staring at the desk, the happy one, the saint who finds good in all creatures. It's the job of the mouth to ask questions, anything to keep the teacher from the boring lesson.

—Frank McCourt, Pulitzer Prize–winning author and
former New York City public high school teacher for 30 years

It is a constant struggle to gain respect for teachers.
—Ron Clark, Disney Teacher of the Year, 2001

The world is full of people who can do, but can't teach. We can.
—Albert Foshry, teacher

... the only thing you need to know about a teacher is whether the kids are learning.
—Chester Fine, Jr., U. S. secretary of
education and president of
Fordham Foundation

We must restore teaching to its rightful status as a profession. We must give our teachers the respect and support they need to accomplish the awesome mission they have been given. For too long, we have taken for granted their dedication and hard work. We have given them greater and greater responsibilities and thanked them less and less.
—Terry Knecht,
former National Teacher of the Year

Teachers leave footprints on the souls of children.
—Unknown

Not many of you should become teachers, my brothers and sisters, for you know that we who teach will be judged with a greater strictness.
—The Bible, James 3:1

Teacher's Creed: We, the unwilling, led by the unqualified, have been doing the unbelievable for so long for so little, we now attempt the impossible with nothing.

—Source unknown

Low morale, depressed, feeling unfairly blamed for the ills of society? You must be a teacher.

—*New York Times*, Education Supplement

The role of the teachers remains the highest calling of a free people.

—Shirley Hufstedler U. S. congresswoman,
former U. S. secretary of education

In a completely rational society, the best of us would aspire to be teachers and the rest of us would settle for something less.

—Lee Iacocca, auto industry magnate (CEO, Chrysler
Corporation), author, and TV commercial actor

Goodbye tension, hello pension!

—Fay Michaud, retiring teacher

To teach is to learn twice.

—Joseph Joubert, musical accompanist,
director, arranger, producer, and orchestrator

I am not a teacher, but an awakener.

—Robert Frost, poet

Principal to teacher: "Your assignment, should you accept, is to increase educational standards while support services dwindle."

—*The Lighter Side of Educational Leadership* by Aaron Bacall

One good teacher in a lifetime may sometimes change a delinquent into a solid citizen.

—Philip Wylie, author

The best teacher . . . is the one who kindles an inner fire, arouses moral enthusiasm, inspires the student with a vision of what he may become. . . .

—Harold Garnett

The best teacher is the one who suggests rather than dogmatizes, and inspires his listener with the wish to teach himself.

—Edward Bulwer-Lytton, British novelist

Why am I a teacher? Because I'm good at it! I choose it!

—Ramona Greschel, teacher

I touch the future, I teach.

—Christa McAuliffe, teacher-astronaut

Teachers can change lives with just the right mix of chalk and challenge.

—Joyce A. Myers, writer

Test:

1. Name 3 supermodels

2. Name 3 of your kid's teachers.

⌒⌒⌒

Know what really matters.

—Sign from the National
PTA Ad Council

⌒⌒⌒

Great teachers never stop.

—Bill Walton, legendary coach and
Basketball Hall of Famer, writing in *USA Weekend*

⌒⌒⌒

Teachers are seed planters.

—Tom Keating, 2004 Minnesota Teacher of the Year

⌒⌒⌒

Teachers are messengers from the past and an escort to the future.

—Albert Einstein, physicist

⌒⌒⌒

It's not that we make a difference—we make the difference for the future.

—Bill Harris, classroom teacher

⌒⌒⌒

A good teacher is better than a barrelful of books.

—Chinese proverb

⌒⌒⌒

Retiring Teacher's Prayer:

The view from the hill is broad and beckoning for indeed we are twice blessed for we are teachers. . . . Our world has suffered little children to come unto us and through them, we have come to know heaven.

—Dorothy Druckemiller, educator

We are all pupils and we are all teachers.

—Gilbert Highet, Scottish-born American classicist, author of *The Art of Teaching*

The Lord has given me the tongue of a teacher, that I may know how to sustain the weary with a word.

—The Bible, James 3:1

A call to all teachers—somebody needs you. America needs you.

—Larry Bell, former U. S. secretary of education

I beg you to stop apologizing for being a member of the most important profession in the world.

—William G. Carr, writer

I know it sounds kind of trite, but if I didn't need a paycheck to survive, I would do this for free. There are so many teachers who feel that way about the profession.

—Maria Frontain, former Arizona Teacher of the Year

To be a teacher in the right sense is to be a learner. I am not a teacher, only a fellow student.

—Søren Kierkegaard, nineteenth-century Danish philosopher and theologian, a founder of existentialism

I've come to the frightening conclusion that I am the decisive factor in the classroom. It is my personal approach that creates the climate. It is my daily mood that creates the weather. I can be a tool of torture or an instrument of inspiration.

—Haim Ginot, teacher and author

Teachers are the soldiers of democracy. Others can defend democracy, but teachers create it.

—General Omar Bradley, World War II Army commander and hero

Teachers have a tremendous impact on student's lives. These role models help students get a direction for their future.

—Harvey McKay, CEO, author, and motivational speaker

I teach because I search.

—Paulo Freire, twentieth-century Brazilian educationalist and author

Teachers need to be differentiated in terms of their talents.

—Joe Klein, chancellor, New York City Schools

I became a teacher because I wanted to help the underdog.

—Elizabeth Bowler, English as a Second Language Teacher of the Year, Yorktown Heights, New York, 2001

A teacher makes two ideas where only one grew before.

—Elbert Hubbard, American writer

No one should teach who is not a bit awed by the importance of the profession.

—George E. Frazier

❧

The best teacher can pan gold in unlikely water.

—Jay Parini, professor, Middleburg College

❧

One good schoolmaster is worth a thousand priests.

—Robert G. Ingersoll, American orator

❧

Better than a thousand days of diligent study is one day with a great teacher.

—Japanese proverb

❧

School teachers are not fully appreciated by parents until it rains all day on Saturday.

—E. C. McKenzie, American humorist and writer

❧

I'm not going to be a movie star. But then, in all probability, Liz Taylor is never going to teach first and second grade.

—Mary J. Wilson, teacher

❧

A teacher is a child's third parent.

—Helen Maxwell Berston, American educator

❧

A good teacher, like a good entertainer, first must hold his audience's attention. Then he can teach his lesson.

—John Henrik Clarke,
American poet, writer, and editor

❧

The most significant word in teacher is "each."
                                        —Robert DeBruyn, author

There's no better word in the language I revere more than "teacher." My heart sings when a kid refers to me as his teacher, and it always has. I've honored myself and the entire family of man by becoming a teacher.
                                —Pat Conroy, author, *Prince of Tides* (1986)

Teachers are more than any other class the guardians of civilization.
                                —Bertrand Russell, British philosopher,
                                        mathematician, and writer

A good teacher is never done with their preparation—grading, evaluating, planning—because they are always trying to reinvent, improve, and inspire.
                                —David Carlson, professor, Duke University

Teachers are the last bastion against darkness and ignorance.
                                —James W. Morris, fifth-grade teacher in Georgia

A teacher's day is half crisis, half monotony, and one-eighth epiphany. Never mind the arithmetic.
                                        —Susan Ohanian, teacher

The task of the teacher is not to work for the pupil nor to oblige him to work, but to show him how to work.
                                —Wanda Landowska, Polish-French musician

I have never heard anyone whom I consider a good teacher claim that he or she is a good teacher . . . self-doubt seems very much a part of the job . . . one can never be sure how well it is going.

—Joseph Epstein

You can't stop a teacher when they want to do something. They just do it.

—J. D. Salinger, author, *Catcher in the Rye*

Teachers are expected to reach unattainable goals with inadequate tools. The miracle is that at times they accomplish this impossible task.

—Haim G. Ginot, teacher and author

Legendary teachers are life-touchers.

—David Scheidecker and
William Freeman, authors

Acquire new knowledge whilst thinking over the old and you may become a teacher of others.

—Confucius, Chinese philosopher

The mediocre teacher tells. The good teacher explains. The superior teacher demonstrates. The great teacher inspires.

—William Arthur Ward, author

We teach what we need to learn.

—Alan Cohen, author

Never underestimate the power of the classroom teacher.
—Aleno Christiano, teacher, teacher of
teachers, lecturer, and writer

I admire the teachers who listen, and the listeners who teach.
—Jodi Hills, author, *I Am Amazed*

Teachers must define the capacity of individual children and
be the midwives of American democracy at the same time.
—Hank Rubin, author

Professional educators are not like medical supply sales
people or astronauts or country singers. Teachers help to
shape lives in a way so special and unique that every single
one of us is irreplaceable. That's an important part of why I
am an educator.
—Leonard O. Pellicer, dean of School of
Education and Organizational Leadership,
University of La Vern

Teachers of the twenty-first century will be village builders.
—Hank Rubin, author

All good teachers have a playful heart.

—Anonymous

If you think that one individual can't make a difference in the
world, consider what one cigar can do on a nine-room house.
—Bill Vaughn, writer

An important personal quality for a teacher is that he cares about humanity. If he doesn't, he is taking his pay illegally.
—Edward C. Helwick, educator

Good teachers never teach anything. What they do is create the conditions under which learning takes place.
—S. I. Hayakawa, philologist, educator, and legislator

Teachers open the door. You enter yourself.
—Chinese proverb

What the teacher is is more important than what he teaches.
—Karl Menninger, psychiatrist and founder of the famed Menninger Clinic in Topeka, Kansas

Teachers are true heroes. Police and firefighters save lives, but teachers save civilization.
—Anonymous

Teachers have to become good public relations experts . . . we have to be advocates for ourselves.
—Philip Bigler, former National Teacher of the Year

Good teachers cost a lot, but poor teachers cost a lot more.
—Evan Esar, humorist

Education helps you earn more. But not many schoolteachers can prove it.
—E. C. McKenzie, American humorist ands writer

A person wasn't a teacher because they had been elected or got a certificate. They were a teacher because they knew something and were respected. If they didn't know enough, they weren't teachers. Or if we didn't need to know what they know, we didn't go to them. I would rather we had this old way.

—Indian elder in *Neither Wolf nor Dog* by Kent Nerburn

Successful teachers are effective in spite of the psychological theories they suffer under.

—Educational proverb

Teachers change people—inside and outside.

—Anonymous

Teachers are in an unenviable position. Like social workers, their job is never really done. There are no clear criteria to indicate when work is over. In teaching, products are never finished, patients never cured, cases never closed.

—Andy Hargreaves, Boston College, educator-author

A great teacher never strives to explain his vision. He simply invites you to stand beside him and see it for yourself.

—R. Inman, author

We . . . owe our teachers a great gift—not another empty "teacher appreciation" day or "teacher of the year" award, but a gift . . . that will help them renew their spirit so they can continue to serve our children and our world well.

—Parker J. Palmer, founder, Fetzer Institute Teacher Formation Program

There is no real teacher who in practice does not believe in the existence of the soul, or in a magic that acts on it through speech.
—Allan Bloom, philosopher and academic

. . . good teachers make the best of a pupil's means; great teachers foresee a pupil's ends.
—Maria Callas, operatic soprano

Last year's Teacher of the Year isn't really as important as this year's teacher of the moment.
—Unknown

Teachers must have vocal cords of steel since many people still hear their favorite teacher speaking to them years after graduation.
—Anonymous

Good teachers are those who know how little they know. Bad teachers are those who think they know more than they don't know.
—Giuseppe Verdi, Italian composer

Teachers are people who start things they never see finished, and for which they never get thanks until it's too late.
—Max Forman, special education consultant

Bad herdsmen ruin their flocks.
—Homer, Greek epic poet

If you can read this, thank a teacher.

—Bumper sticker

Those who love the young the best stay young longest.

—Edgar Friedenberg

A successful teacher needs: the education of a college president, the executive ability of a financier, the humanity of a deacon, the adaptability of a chameleon, the hope of an optimist, the courage of a hero, the wisdom of a serpent, the gentleness of a dove, the patience of Job, the grace of God, and the persistence of the devil.

—Unknown

I put the relation of a fine teacher to a student just below the relation of a mother to a son.

—Thomas Wolfe, writer and playwright

In a world where change is the norm, our teachers are sources of constancy, mentors who guide us and let us see the future.

—Mary Rodarte, author-educator

What constitutes the teacher is the passion to make scholars.

—George Herbert Palmer,
American scholar and educator

Few statements on quality education deal with teachers' needs in day-to-day school operation. Teachers, apparently, are taken for granted as a part of the classroom scenery, like desks, chairs, and books.

—J. Lloyd Trump, educator-author

We challenge you to make the best people you can by being the best teachers you are able to be.

—David Scheidecker and
William Freeman, educator-authors

Classroom teachers give young people what they sometimes get nowhere else in society—a sense that they have promise, that they have talents, that they are special. If you're a young person who is not quite sure that you are welcome in this society, one of the most important people in your life could be a teacher who accepts you.

—Parker J. Palmer, founder, Fetzer
Institute Teacher Formation Program

Life is amazing; and the teacher had better prepare himself to be a medium for that amazement.

—Edward Blishen, writer

The most creative and emotionally engaged teachers see themselves not just as educating learners and workers, but as developing citizens.

—Andy Hargreaves and
Michael Fullan, educator-authors

Effective teachers manage. Ineffective teachers discipline.

—Harry Wong, educational consultant

As teachers, we must constantly try to improve schools and we must keep working at changing and experimenting and trying until we have developed ways of reaching every child.

—Albert Shanker, teacher union organizer,
president of the American Federation of Teachers (AFT)

Teachers should guide without dictating, and participate without dominating.

—L. B. Neblette, American teacher

c ✄ ᗞ

Good teachers are glad when a term begins and a little sad when it ends.

—Margaret Mead, anthropologist and author

c ✄ ᗞ

The teaching goes on.

—Mitch Albom, author,
Tuesdays With Morrie

c ✄ ᗞ

Movie stars and rock musicians, athletes and models aren't heroes, they're celebrities. Heroes abound in public schools, a fact that doesn't make the news.

—Frosty Troy, quoted in
Oklahoma Observer, 2001

c ✄ ᗞ

We schoolmasters must temper discretion with deceit.

—Evelyn Waugh, author-educator

c ✄ ᗞ

For a teacher, old age arrives every year.

—Tracy Kidder, Pulitzer
Prize–winning author

c ✄ ᗞ

Bad teaching wastes a good deal of effort and spoils many lives which might have been full of energy and happiness.

—Unknown

c ✄ ᗞ

Teachers, who educate children, deserve more honor than parents who merely give them birth; for the latter provided mere life, while the former ensure a good life.

—Aristotle, Greek philosopher

Success for a teacher means motivating students to believe that they are smart—not stupid—and helping students develop self-images that will lift them to heights they had never dreamed of before.

—Lily Poonawalla, educator from India

The teachers . . . may not be celebrities in the usual sense, but in a very real way they are the ultimate celebrities, leading lives for which we should all be grateful, lives that we should truly celebrate.

—Michael D. Eisner, CEO, Disney Corporation

All good teachers go to heaven. God needs someone to take attendance.

—Unknown

If the government gives out medals to heroes who infiltrate hostile terrain, survive repeated missile attacks, and demonstrate bravery by turning their backs on the enemy, every teacher in the country should get one. Substitute teachers should get two.

—Robert D. Ramsey, author,
What Matters Most for School Leaders

It is the supreme art of the teacher to awaken joy in creative expression and knowledge.

—Albert Einstein, physicist

As teachers, we have a chance to leave our thumbprint on children's lives. Let that thumbprint be that we made a difference.

—John Blaydes, educator,
motivational speaker, and author

The good teacher is someone who can understand those not very good at explaining and explain to those not very good at understanding.

—W. A. Palmer, author

Good teachers have a toehold on immortality.

—John Keasler

Teachers—two kinds: The kind that fills you with so much quail shot that you can't move, and the kind that just gives you a little prod behind and you jump to the skies.

—Robert Frost, poet

Great teachers don't tell us what we see but remind us to open our eyes.

—Anonymous

You can pay people to teach, but you can't pay them to care.

—Marva Collins

The best of teachers are those who have labored to be understood by the dullest capacities.

—Charles H. Spurgeon, British
preacher and author

The only thing more expensive than a good teacher is the price a community pays for an ineffective one.

—Arlene Greco, Christian author

America's teachers are the culture heroes of our time. Daily they are asked to solve problems that baffle the rest of us. Daily they are asked to work with resources nowhere near commensurate with the task. And daily they are berated by politicians, the public and the press for their alleged failures and inadequacies.

—Parker J. Palmer, founder, Fetzer Institute
Teacher Formation Program

The teacher who is indeed wise does not bid you to enter the house of his wisdom but leads you to the threshold of your mind.

—Kahlil Gibran, Syrian-born American
mystic poet, painter, and author of *The Prophet*

No one ever got to be a better teacher who wasn't working on being a better person.

—Noah ben Shea, poet, philosopher, scholar, humorist,
lecturer, business consultant, and best-selling author

The influence of a genuine educator lies in what he is rather than what he says.

—Oswald Spengler, German philosopher

Have you ever really had a teacher? One who saw you as a raw but precious thing, a jewel that, with wisdom, could be polished to a proud shine.

—Mitch Albom, in *Tuesdays With Morrie*

Teachers believe they have a gift for giving; it drives them
with the same irrepressible drive that drives other to create a
work of art or a market or a building.

> —A. Bartlett Giamatti, Yale professor and
> former major league baseball commissioner

I think I was actually born to be a teacher. And I think I never
stopped being a teacher—thinking like a teacher, in all the
time I was lieutenant governor. . . . I love it, I really do.

> —Mae Schunk, Minnesota lieutenant
> governor under Governor Jesse Ventura

The teacher's life should have three periods—study until
twenty-five, investigation until forty, profession until sixty, at
which age I would have him retire on a double allowance.

> —Sir William Osler, Canadian physician

A teacher must believe in the value and interest of his subject
as a doctor believes in health.

> —Gilbert Highet, Scottish-born American
> classicist, author of *The Art of Teaching*

The real teachers of the year are those who report to school
each day despite physical threat to their safety; or teachers
who don't lose their enthusiasm for teaching even when they
are surrounded by tired and pessimistic colleagues.

> —Andy Baumgarten, former
> National Teacher of the Year

"In my job, I had to be at work early, stay late, and take work
home. I had to produce, manufacture, invent, salvage, transport,
motivate, assess, create, congratulate, and challenge. My job

combined the skills of psychoanalyst, chauffeur, chef, artist, doctor, scientist, mathematician, coach, musician, and professional wrestler." "What were you called?" . . . came the inevitable question. Pulling herself up to her full height, she replied with satisfaction, "I was called . . . Teacher."

—Except from *To Share a Life* by Melissa Fornay, 1952

Anyone who has ever spent two hours overseeing a child's birthday party gets a glimpse of what a teacher needs to know.

—Dave Eggers, Daniel Moulthrop, and Ninive Clements Calegari, authors of *Teachers Have It Easy*

Teachers don't merely have real-time impact. They have virtually timeless impact.

—Anonymous

I did become a teacher and those experiences are among the most important of my life.

—Laura Bush, first lady and former elementary teacher and librarian

You have chosen to be a teacher and what you will get out of being a teacher is your choice. Teaching is a demanding career which will not lead to great riches or fame. It is also a challenging and rewarding career which can bring you great joy. You will—every day—teach and change the lives of your students because when they learn something new, everything they know changes a little.

—Alene Christiano, teacher, teacher of teachers, lecturer, and author

I am a teacher at heart, and there are moments in the classroom when I can hardly hold my joy . . . when the pathway out of a thicket opens up before us, when our experience is illuminated by the lightning and life of the mind—then teaching is the finest work I know.

—Parker J. Palmer, founder, Fetzer
Institute Teacher Formation Program

. . . you don't feel like a person when you're teaching. It feels like being a train.

—Julia Normand, English teacher in Alaska

You quietly get the job done, and you do so with incredible dedication, perseverance, and dignity in an environment of steadily diminishing resources and escalating criticisms of schools. Why do you do it? I believe the answer is very simple. You love children. You want to give children the best possible start in life.

—Nancy Keenans, Montana
State Department of Education

Forget that foolish saying, Those who can, do; and those who can't, teach. Not only is this statement derogatory and insulting to the dedicated professional in education and training, but with few exceptions, it just ain't so. The reality? Those who do best teach best.

—Mark Sanborn, motivational speaker and writer

It's not the books. It's not the buses. It's not the bleachers. It's the teachers!

—A. C. Wharton, mayor, Shelby County, Tennessee

I am a teacher! What I do and say are being absorbed by young minds who will echo these images across the ages. My lessons will be immortal, affecting people yet unborn, people I will never see or know. The future of the world is in my classroom today. . . .

Only a teacher? Thank God I have a calling to the greatest profession of all. I must be vigilant every day lest I lose one fragile opportunity to improve tomorrow.

—Ivan Welton Fitzwater, teacher

Most of the significant advances in civilization have been the result of the work of teachers.

—James Marran, Social Studies Department Chair,
New Trier High School, Winnetka, Illinois

Tributes and Testimonials

5

Americans struggle with two diametrically opposing views of their schools and their teachers. Many people subscribe to the popular notion that the nation's schools (and by implication the teaching profession) are falling short. Yet at the same time—almost universally—parents and students testify that their school and teachers are superior—or better!

Of the two views, the tributes and testimonials ring most true because they are based on real-world personal experience and firsthand knowledge of results.

The most credible witness to the worthiness of any service profession and its practitioners is what customers say about them. And when it comes to customer kudos, teachers take the prize. They receive more positive tributes and testimonials than all other professional groups put together.

Not many people give unsolicited, glowing testimonials of praise to their lawyer. Or chiropractor. Or hairdresser. Or tax preparer. But, sooner or later, most of us heap praise on the teacher(s) who helped define and prepare us for our life path.

For those looking for proof that teaching is the nation's highest calling, testimonials say it best. Fortunately, tributes for teachers are never difficult to find. Following is a representative sampling of typical testimonials to individual teachers and to the profession as a whole.

Many people feel moved to thank the teachers that mean so much to them. Never is this more readily observed than through the sentiments expressed during National Teacher Appreciation Week. . . . Appreciation comes in all sizes and shapes. . . . Even a cursory look at the sentiments that gushed forth from institutions, individuals, and the media during teacher appreciation week can provide a wealth of inspiration for the job-seeking teacher. Keep at it. We need you.

—Sarah Sawyer, freelance writer

Behind every actress, chef, author, and race car driver is one special person who offered crucial life lessons.

—Unnamed *Life* magazine writer, August 19, 2005

I was greatly influenced by one of my teachers. She had a zeal not so much for perfection as for steady betterment—she demanded not excellence as much as integrity.

—Edward R. Murrow, journalist and news commentator

To a special person in my life: Thank you for reaching deep into the corners of my being and seeing a part of me I did not know existed and others never saw. Thank you for your faith in my abilities and my future when I did not believe. Thank you for sharing a part of your humanity and for the spark that glows warmly inside me. Thank you. Your influence is etched in my soul forever.

—Susan Parks,
school administrator

The teacher who had the most profound effect on what would become a life's passion was my twelfth-grade English teacher, Mr. Bower. His enthusiasm for the English language was inspirational and contagious. "Gather words," he told us, "as one might gather a bouquet of flowers. Breathe into your soul their fragrance and embrace their intrinsic power to enlighten your spirit and soar your imagination."

I applaud his dedication and envision how pleased he would be to know that because of his extraordinary influence on me, I have published a novel and two children's books; I am working on my second novel; and I am also the publisher of *Stressfree Living* magazine. God bless you, Mr. Bower!

—T. J. Stelten, author, editor, and publisher

We are grateful to all dedicated teachers, who are the heroes of all time.

—Gretchen Kresl Hassler (teacher) and Jon
Hassler (author and professor)

I am quite certain that in the hereafter she will take me by the hand and lead me to my proper seat.

—Bernard Baruch, financier and statesman,
writing about one of his early teachers

I had a third grade teacher named Mrs. Phillips. She was about 3 feet tall and powdered her face with something that smelled just like cookies. Every day after school, we would line up at the door and kiss her cheek goodbye. Can you imagine that happening today?

She read to us constantly—grown-up literature as well as kid's books. She would blindly open a dictionary and point to our new word of the day. She had us writing imagery when rain streaked down our classroom windows. In the winter, she played classical music in the background while we read. A couple of us noticed that she cried at that time of year and later learned that her son (an only child) had been killed on Christmas Eve.

Mrs. Phillips never talked down to a child or assumed they were anything other than brilliant. She had no need to raise her voice because we felt it was an honor to be trusted by her (she could leave the room for 20 minutes and not worry about chaos).

Why am I sharing all this with you? Because I think an inspirational book about teachers' impact on our lives would be wonderful. It got me to thinking about Mrs. Phillips, and Mr. Ross, and Mr. Layton, and so many others who had faith in a shy skinny kid with freckles.

—Anonymous national sales
director for a major publisher

Whoever coined the phrase, "You are the wind beneath my wings," most assuredly was reflecting on the sublime influence of a very special teacher.

—Unknown

My ode to Mr. Houlihan and Miss Green—All of us fondly recall our favorite teachers . . . two individuals readily come to mind . . . because both had a tremendous impact on a boy growing up in the fifties in Valley Stream, Long Island,

New York. They were very different in age, gender, how and what they taught, and how they related to students. They were also similar in two respects: they loved children and they loved to teach them. In addition, they were excellent examples of two traits that define expert teachers: enthusiasm and caring.

—Robert Hohn, professor of
Education, University of Kansas

We cannot enter a learning society, an education age, without giving teachers the recognition they deserve.

—Federico Mayo, UNESCO
Director-General, 1987–1994

My mother was an elementary teacher so I grew up with the notion that teachers get to not only touch but create the future in ways that others can only imagine. I love to volunteer in classes in whatever capacity they will have me. So here's my story.

I was in a first-grade classroom and the lesson of the day was the First Movement of Beethoven's 5th Symphony. I played the piece, discussed it, and talked about Beethoven's life. I explained that he was deaf and never actually heard most of the wonderful music he created. . . . I cannot imagine anyone living in the Western Hemisphere, not having been exposed to it. As I was packing to leave, one little boy turned to his teacher and said, "Wow, that was really cool music. I've never heard that before." Wow, indeed, I thought. Now he has. . . .

Teachers are very lucky; they get to tell stories like that.

—Jeffrey W. Jacobs, mayor, St. Louis Park, Minnesota

She (Chris Zejoc) belonged among children. They made her confront sorrow and injustice. They made her feel useful.

Again this year, some had needed more help than she could provide. There were many problems that she hadn't solved. But it wasn't for lack of trying. She hadn't given up. She had run out of time.

—Tracy Kidder, Pulitzer Prize–winning author

When I think of my favorite teachers, Mrs. Matheney, my first-grade teacher, immediately comes to mind. She was a dedicated teacher who sought to instill in her students a love for learning.

For her, a reading or math lesson was never just a means to teach us about sentence structure or addition; instead they were ways to get us excited about learning. I remember our group reading activities fondly.

My favorite part was how Mrs. Matheney made things concrete. We never simply read the stories, we also acted them out . . . we used cardboard boxes to paint and create houses and forests, pipe cleaners to make flowers, and scrap fabrics to make hats and scarves. During these activities, we learned more about math and science than we ever did in any formal lesson. As a class, we had to figure out what paint colors to mix together to make purple and how many more apples we needed if we only had two and the story called for six.

Mrs. Matheney was an amazing teacher, not simply because she taught us to become good readers, but because she made learning fun and motivated us to work hard to learn the skills we needed to become lifelong learners. . . .

—Karrie Shogren, special education
doctoral candidate (quoted in
The Jayhawk, summer 2005)

As with all great teachers, his curriculum was an insignificant part of what he communicated. From him, you didn't learn a subject, but life. Tolerance and justice, fearlessness and pride, reverence and pity are learned in a course on long division if the teacher has these qualities.

—William Alexander Percy, writer

I had an English teacher our sophomore year whom we loved, a large long-haired woman named Sue who wore purple almost exclusively and was a friendly hippie sort. She was one of the best teachers I ever had. Her hair fell to her chair like a puppet-show curtain. She made you want to be a teacher, to throw the light on for children that way.

—Anne Lamott, author

You know them. We all do. The teacher who made a difference. That coach we'll never forget. The music teacher or Sunday school worker who helped us believe in ourselves. We all remember people who shaped our lives in various ways. People whose influence changed us. . . . Who are the un-thanked people from your past? It may not be too late to say, "Thanks."

—Steve Goodier, minister and
national radio personality (1930s)

We're lucky if there's been a teacher who was there for us. Someone who changed our lives. Someone who taught us about values. Someone who challenged us. Someone who made us better than we thought we could be. Someone whose words will stick with us for a lifetime. . . . Thank you teachers everywhere.

—Rob Peluso, artistic director, Minnesota History Theatre

Last year a teacher came to me about a student in her math class. He wasn't turning in his work and she wanted a conference with the parents. The parents did not speak English, so this teacher found an interpreter and called a conference at a time when both parents could attend. The end result was a student who started turning in his work. No other teacher, including myself, went to the length this almost-retired teacher did to reach that student. That teacher did not have her foot out the door—it was firmly planted in her classroom. Teachers like her are the rule rather than the exception. . . .

—Beth Stenglein, a fellow teacher in a letter to the editor

We are what we are because of our teachers.

—Viney Kirpal, executive president of the Global Research Education and Training Foundation (GREAT)

One looks back with appreciation to the brilliant teachers . . . with gratitude to those who touched our human feelings.

—Carl Jung, Swiss psychologist

The year was 1931, and I was a ten-year-old sixth grader. My teacher had a windup Victrola phonograph and a few 78 rpm records. One day she played a recording unlike anything I had ever heard before. It was a woman singing a beautiful classical number which I later came to know as "Who Is Sylvia?" The concert artist was Italian opera star, Galli-Curci. The solo voice with piano accompaniment immediately captivated me. Something in me responded. I knew this was for me.

That was the first time I was exposed to classical music. My mother and dad were both born and raised on Swedish farms; classical music was not part of their experience.

During the next few years I sought out opportunities to hear more of this kind of music. It soon became a passion of mine, leading to some 75 years of seeking out classical music

of all kinds. . . . It all started because a sixth grade teacher created an environment that caught my attention, opening a
completely new dimension of life for me. Galli-Curci became
a friend of mine. I am forever grateful.
—Roland S. Larson, retired educator
and workshop trainer

In 1938, with the completion of the Central High School, the
school board hired its first art teacher, Mildred Dudding. She
had just graduated from college and this was her first job. And
she looked it. She was young and attractive. Anyone who did
not know she was a teacher easily mistook her for one of the
students. . . .

After she was hired, the superintendent, Leland F. Leland,
introduced her at a student assembly. When he asked if anyone
would be interested in taking an art class, all the boys stood up.

"Miss Dudding, I was one of those boys."
—Bob Reiss, local historian (2005)

As adults, when we think back to our years in school, we
remember teachers, not instructional methods and techniques.
We remember teachers who . . . made a connection, planting
those cherished memories, and good feelings that continue to
live within us whoever we are or whatever we become.
—John Blaydes, educator,
author, and motivational speaker

Dear Mrs. Respek, Whenever I see a potato I think of you.
—Thank-you note from a second-grade
pupil to a volunteer teacher whose lesson on
"Respect" required students to "adopt" a potato

The great Vive Kanand had once asked, "You might have lost sleep over so many personal worries, have you ever lost sleep over your country?" I believe he was the great teacher he was because he lost sleep over his subject.

—Kud lu Chitprabha, Indian educator

Our students weren't always able to tell us how much we were needed and appreciated. At times, they would protest when we pushed them to reach their potential. Still, they told us over and over again in their own way they were glad we had been there.

This was never clearer to me than my last year of teaching. I was too young (in my late 50s) when I was forced to leave the profession I loved. Because of some rather harsh after-effects from cancer treatments, I was too weak to continue my career. Just before the end of the year, I came back to visit our class. I was welcomed like a returning monarch. It was heartwarming, but the crowning moment came when I walked out of our room to find a group of boys waiting for me. They wanted to escort me down the hall so no one would accidentally bump into me! No queen ever had more honored guards. This is the picture I would like to pass on to teachers everywhere as a symbol of what they mean to their students and what students would express to them if given the opportunity.

—Carol Ann Larson, retired teacher,
author, activist, and cancer survivor

Marge Hooley wasn't always the most popular teacher among her peers or the administration, but she was among parents—and among kids. Perhaps to the embarrassment of some other staff members, literally all families wanted their children to be in her third-grade class. For good reason.

Her classroom featured reading lofts, activity and interest centers, and individual study areas, and was always buzzing with excitement. She wasn't afraid to bend rules to go to bat for her kids.

Marge Hooley made teaching look easy. But her success was rooted in hard work, long hours, and a heavy emotional investment.

Did she do it for the money? I don't think so. You see, at the end of each school year, the district's business manager always complained, because she hadn't cashed her paychecks. They weren't lost. They were just carefully stashed in a dresser drawer for safekeeping.

For Marge Hooley, as for many teachers, money is not the greatest reward in teaching.

—Robert D. Ramsey, educator-author

A promising high school senior, looking forward to a career in Spanish education, became discouraged and dropped out of school. Instead of graduating, she went to work as a waitress in a local restaurant.

One day, the girl spied her previous favorite English teacher entering the restaurant where she worked. The young girl tried to avoid the teacher, but the teacher saw her and confronted her asking, "What are you doing here?" The girl confessed that she was a dropout.

The teacher took her former pupil by the hand, looked in her eyes and said, "My dear, you will make a wonderful teacher. You must pursue your dream."

The girl followed through. Graduated. Became a successful Spanish teacher and helped found a pioneering Spanish immersion school. The student, now grown, recounted this vignette upon receiving a distinguished alumni award from the very alma mater she once dropped out of.

—As told by Bob Tift, president,
Benilde-St. Margaret's Junior and Senior High Schools

When Glen Sorenson from Proctor was named 2005 Minnesota Teacher of the Year, he said, "Now, I just need about 70,000 more of these for all the teachers in the state."

I can't stop thinking about his words because they are so true, especially here. . . . Every one of our 340 teachers deserves praise and recognition for a job well done.

Like Mr. Sorenson, I wish I had 340 awards to present. Each of our teachers deserves one.

—Debra Bower, suburban superintendent

Tina is a school social worker who serves four small school districts. She loves her kids, spends her own money to help them sometimes, and makes every effort to provide a support system which is almost always lacking in their nonschool life (e.g., some live in dysfunctional families and homes with broken windows and trash in the yard).

Even in the small towns of Kansas, she deals every day with child abuse (both sexual and physical), poverty, health problems, and deprivation beyond what most of us can imagine.

I am reminded of the W. B. Yeats poem, *The Lake Isle of Innisfree*. A quote from one line reads, "And I shall have some peace there, for peace comes dropping." Yeats spoke of a place of solitude and peace where a beleaguered person could seek solace from the chaos and distraction of life.

Tina, without being fully aware of it, is helping her students seek their "Innisfree."

—Owen M. Henson, educational administrator,
Emporia State University, Kansas

In addition to the resources, the technology, the facilities, and the programs that were available at Park [high school], it was the teachers that made my education rich, challenging, and

powerful. . . . I was nurtured, pushed, challenged, brought to task, taught over and over to compromise, forgive myself, forgive others, and teased with cleverness, humor, creativity, and compassion. So many teachers were role models and friends. . . .
—Marj Youmans, valedictorian, St. Louis
Park (MN) High School, 2002

A woman attended her 20-year high school reunion. There she encountered her freshman art teacher. She told him that she decided to go to college as a result of his inspiration and that she was an art professor now at a large state university.

At the end of the evening's festivities, the teacher searched out his former student, shook her hand, and said, "Thank you for saying those nice things about my teaching. You really made my day."

"You're welcome," said the woman, as she hugged him. "But let me thank you—you made my life."
—Author unknown quoted in *You Moved
My Life: Heartwarming Stories of Teachers Who
Mentored and Taught Us to Dream* by Viney Kirpal

I had a very special teacher in high school many years ago whose husband died suddenly of a heart attack. About a week after his death, she shared some of her insights.

With a gentle look of reflection on her face, she paused and said, "Class is over. I would like to share with all of you a thought that is unrelated to class, but which I feel is very important.

Each of us is put on earth to learn, share, love, appreciate, and give of ourselves. None of us knows when that fantastic experience will end. . . .

So I would like you to make me a promise. From now on, on your way to school, or on your way home, find something beautiful to notice. It doesn't have to be something you see, it can be a scent, perhaps of freshly baked bread wafting out of someone's home, or it could be the sound of a breeze slightly rustling the leaves. . . .

Please look at these things and cherish them . . . these are the stuff of life. The little things we are put on earth to enjoy. The things we often take for granted."

The class was completely quiet. We all picked up our books and filed out of the room silently. That afternoon, I noticed more things on the way home from school than I had the whole semester.

Every once in a while, I think of that teacher and remember what an impression she made on all of us, and I try to appreciate all of those things that sometimes we all overlook.

—According to an anonymous source on the
Internet, Lisa Beamer—wife of Todd Beamer
who said, "Let's roll," and helped bring down
a hijacked plane headed for Washington, DC, on
September 11th—told this story on *Good Morning America*

Throughout his distinguished career as a teacher, principal and associate superintendent in Topeka, Kansas, Dr. Owen Henson received many awards and accolades. But one of the honors that meant the most to him was an invitation to deliver the commencement address to the graduating class of his former high school in Elwood, Kansas.

When the time to give the speech came around, Henson's first words were not directed to the graduates. Instead they were addressed to Monica Schoeneck, his former 1st grade teacher, who was seated in the audience.

Now, over 100 years old, Mrs. Schoeneck had concluded a 52-year career, most of it as an elementary teacher in Elwood.

Henson began his commencement address by thanking her for giving him the greatest gift of all—the gift of reading! Without that gift, Henson said, none of his career success would ever have occurred.

—Robert D. Ramsey, educator-author

When I think back on my favorite teachers, I don't remember anymore much of what they taught me, but I sure remember being excited about learning it.

What has stayed with me are not the facts they imparted, but the excitement about learning they inspired.

—Thomas L. Friedman, Pulitzer Prize–winning
New York Times columnist and author

Teachers who have plugged away at their jobs twenty, thirty, and forty years are heroes. I suspect they know in their hearts they've done a good thing, too, and are more satisfied with themselves than most people are.

Most of us end up with no more than five or six people who remember us. Teachers have thousands of people who remember them for the rest of their lives.

—Andrew J. Rooney, journalist,
writer, and TV curmudgeon

A Final Word:
It's Worth It!

As indicated earlier, today's teachers truly are over-worked, overwhelmed, underpaid, and unappreciated. So why do they do it? The long answer is found throughout the pages of this collection. The short answer is: simply because it's worth it.

Of course, teaching isn't the greatest profession for every-one. Only for those talented and dedicated men and women who make it great by what they do in the classroom every day. It is the greatest profession for all those who teach, not only because they want to, but because they have to. Because it is who they are; it is their calling.

Every year, we give hundreds of prospects a license and a title; but that doesn't make them a true teacher. Great teachers become great teachers because of what they know and do and the respect they earn. For them—and only for them—teaching is, without question, the greatest profession of all . . . for others (wannabes, pretenders, and also-rans) it is only a job.

If you like metaphors, think of the ovenbird (also known as the "teacher bird"), a thrush-like American warbler whose shrill cry sounds like, "Teacher. Teacher. TEACHER!" It is a cry that is unmistakable, persistent, and impossible to ignore—just as the call to teaching is unrelenting and unavoidable for those authentic practitioners of society's most important craft.

Naturally, there are days when teaching is a lousy job, but it is always a noble, honorable, and worthwhile career. Other professions may be safer, saner, more certain, and more secure. But none other deserves the label "the greatest." Rather, for those who care enough and hear the call, teaching stands alone—as life's grandest work.

If you are a teacher, take time some quiet night when you are all alone and listen to the voices of Teachers Past. They will all tell you that when you begin teaching, you want to change the world. And when you stop teaching, you realize that that is exactly what you have done. It's worth it!

Resource A

*Insights and Observations on Teaching
That Only Teachers Will Appreciate*

Teachers work in a special world of their own creation and inhabited by God's most endearing and exasperating creatures—children. Consequently, there are things about the teaching life that no one outside the profession knows or would comprehend and appreciate if they did.

Like all professions, teaching has its own secrets. Following are some of my favorite insights and observations that only teachers will fully understand and appreciate:

- Being a teacher is nothing to sneeze at—except during the cold and flu season, when all the kids do it.
- Teachers pick up where parents leave off. Unfortunately, many parents are leaving off a lot sooner than they used to.
- Going through the school express lunch line is as close to living in the fast lane as many teachers ever get.
- In your grandmother's time, teachers were trained in a "normal" school. Today, prospective teachers would be better served by being trained in an "abnormal" school.
- Nothing feels much better than the precise moment when every student "gets it."
- Teachers are magic. They can help students become different and all alike at the same time.
- Kids are funny. They can break your heart and make your day—all before lunchtime.
- Teaching is tougher today. So are teachers.

- Teachers are sneaky. They'll teach you something while you think you're just having fun.
- Teachers didn't invent "tough love," they just perfected it.
- The worst student you ever had made you a better teacher.
- The most annoying question asked of teachers is, "What do you do all summer?" Have these people ever heard of healing?
- Some people wonder if there is intelligent life on other planets. On some days, every teacher wonders if there is any on this planet.
- Do not ask for whom the bell tolls. It tolls for recess.
- Good teaching is mostly removing obstacles.
- Some days, a fire drill is about the only break teachers get.
- When schools are closed, the whole community feels empty.
- Teachers don't need fancy gimmicks or gadgets. A good teacher can make an entire lesson out of a snowflake.
- No teacher is God. God would never agree to take cafeteria duty.
- If asked would you rather teach a favorite lesson or have good sex, teachers would overwhelmingly choose sex. Teachers are dedicated, not stupid.
- Teaching is a dance you do with your students. And you get to lead.
- SWAT teams have semiautomatic weapons. And security guards have mace and stun guns. But teachers have "the look."
- Who needs therapy as long as you have the teachers' lounge?
- If you need a reason for having sweet dreams, think of your best student. If you need a reason to get out of bed in the morning, think of your worst one.
- If a lesson fails, the teacher still gets paid. The kids get nothing at all.

- It's strange how lonely you can feel in an overcrowded classroom.
- A bad teacher is an insult to the nation's children.
- Like fine tea, a teacher-pupil relationship needs time to steep and mellow to become full-bodied.
- One secret of successful teaching is to never get a really comfortable desk chair.
- Good teaching doesn't require bureaucracy.
- Bad teaching is a form of child abuse.
- Some teachers believe in corporal punishment—but only for bad parents.
- Good teachers love a day off. That's when they catch up on their work.
- Football players have their two-minute drill. So do teachers—it's called lunch.
- Teachers aren't taller than other people. It just seems that way because so many people look up to them.
- You can always tell the most experienced teachers— they don't eat school lunch on meatloaf day.
- A teacher's idea of heaven is a place where there is good pay, good kids, and plenty of time to go to the bathroom.
- There is an unwritten code among teachers: They never tell the principal that he or she doesn't really run the school.

Teaching is a demanding, demeaning, difficult, underpaid occupation. God, don't you just love it?!

Resource B

Other Books That Inspire Teachers

Good teachers can inspire wayward students to refocus, dream anew, and try harder. Good books can do the same thing for flagging teachers. The following works and collections have been known to do just that.

Ben Shea, N. (2002). *Great quotes to inspire great teachers*. Thousand Oaks, CA: Corwin Press.

Canfield, J., Hanson, M. V., & Wohlmuth, S. J. (2003). *Chicken soup of the soul celebrates teachers*. Deerfield Beach, CA: Health Communications.

Caruana, V. (2003). *Apples and chalkdust: Inspirations and encouragements for teachers*. Guilford, CT: The Lyon Press.

Edmundson, M. (2003). *Teacher: The one who made a difference*. New York: Vintage Books.

Eisner, M. D. (2000). *Thank you, teacher: Letters celebrating extraordinary teachers*. New York: Disney Enterprises.

Gangs, C. K., & Patterson, J. (2002). *The gift of teaching: A book of favorite quotations to inspire and encourage*. New York: Barnes & Noble.

Intractor, S. D., & Scribner, M. (2003). *Teaching with fire: Poetry that sustains the courage to teach*. San Francisco: Jossey-Bass.

Ramsey, R. D. (2003). *501 tips for teachers* (2nd ed.). Chicago: Contemporary Books.

Reeves, D. B. (2001). *Crusade in the classroom*. New York: Simon & Schuster.

Schribner, D. (2001). *I remember my teacher: 365 reminiscences of teachers who changed our lives*. Kansas City, MO: Andrews McMeel.

Sell, C. (2004). *A cup of comfort for teachers: Heartwarming stories of people who mentor, motivate, and inspire*. Avon, MA: Adams Media.

**CORWIN
PRESS**

The Corwin Press logo—a raven striding across an open book—represents the union of courage and learning. Corwin Press is committed to improving education for all learners by publishing books and other professional development resources for those serving the field of PreK–12 education. By providing practical, hands-on materials, Corwin Press continues to carry out the promise of its motto: **"Helping Educators Do Their Work Better."**